Unforgettable Sundays That Celebrate Jesus

VOLUME TWO

Creating Life-Changing Worship Services

in a Sight and Sound Culture

by Doug and Melissa Timberlake,
Wenda Shereos,
and Elaine Hurst

MAINSTAY CHURCH RESOURCES
WHEATON, ILLINOIS

A Source Book of Creative Mood Setters and Sermon Boosters

Acquisition editor: Karen Mains.

Produced by The Livingstone Corporation for Mainstay Church Resources. Project staff include Bruce Barton, Jonathan Farrar, Chris Hudson, Linda Taylor, Carol Ochs, and Tom and Kathy Ristow.

Cover and interior design by Gary Gnidovic.

Mainstay Church Resources' passion is to facilitate revival among God's people by helping pastors help people develop healthy spiritual habits in nine vital areas that always characterize genuine times of spiritual awakening. To support this goal, Mainstay Church Resources uses a C.H.U.R.C.H. strategy to provide practical tools and materials, including the annual 50-Day Spiritual Adventure, the Seasonal Advent Celebration, and the Pastor's Toolkit.

Library of Congress Cataloging in Publication Data

Timberlake, Doug and Melissa, and Wenda Shereos, Elaine Hurst

Unforgettable Sundays / Doug and Melissa Timberlake, Wenda Shereos, and Elaine Hurst.

ISBN 1–57849–168–1

08 07 06 05 04 03 02 01 00 99

10 9 8 7 6 5 4 3 2 1

Printed in the United States of America

Dedication

This book is dedicated to Christian artists everywhere who long to advance the kingdom through the use of the arts, and to the Pastors and church leaders who support their passion and vision.

Acknowledgments

We extend special appreciation to the pastors and Unforgettable Sundays Seminar participants who brainstormed ideas with us and spurred us on to develop them fully and put them in writing.

Thank you Randall Mains, for the encouraging role you've played in developing our seminars and this series of books. You've been there taking risks to back this vision, may God reward you greatly.

Karen Mains, thank you for being such a strong voice of encouragement, for forging ahead when we were tired and discouraged, and for gifting us with your writing, conceptualizing, and editing. There is no doubt that this all would not have happened without you!

Special thanks to Leanne Mitchell, the music minister of Hope Evangelical Free Church in Springfield, Illinois, for your contribution of music and worship resources.

Wenda thanks her husband, Bill, for his patience and encouragement to "just be who you are."

Elaine thanks her 9–5 boss, Duane, for flexibility "above and beyond the call" as she worked on this project, and is ESPECIALLY GRATEFUL for her husband, Brad, for his personal sacrifice and support.

Tom and Bev Mascari, you've played an important role in pushing us to follow our dreams! Thanks for encouraging, listening, and being "on call" for fun. Your friendship is and always will be a gift to us. May we continue to "dream big" together.

We are awed that God would choose to give us this opportunity to help the local church point the way to Jesus through the use of creativity and the arts.

Contents

[continued on next page]

Contents

Introduction

"Hi, I'm a pastor from one of the churches here in town. I just read *Unforgettable Sundays* in one sitting—from cover to cover. It's given me such excitement and vision for the future. Could we meet for lunch to discuss some of the ideas? I can hardly wait to use the Mood Setters and Sermon Boosters and was hoping I could get your feedback as I run my thoughts by you."

As we met together and shared insights with this pastor, our team was again affirmed that what we'd written in the first volume of *Unforgettable Sundays* was really working. How exciting to hear continually from people who read *Unforgettable Sundays, Volume 1* and are able to immediately implement the suggestions during their Sunday services. We love to watch the mental light bulbs click on as our suggestions are embraced with positive, "Hey, I can do that!" attitudes. The only hitch came when pastors began requesting even more ideas, which brings us to why we've written *Unforgettable Sundays, Volume Two.*

Obviously, there's a passion among church leaders to make Sundays unforgettable. The problem is that in our sight and sound culture, there's an enormous lack of practical approaches and resources that work in all congregations, no matter how large or small. That's been our heartfelt passion—to help all churches learn to teach one concept through a variety of ways in order to combat society's information overload. We want to gift the church with effective communication tools that are easy to implement, but don't always require a huge budget or a huge staff.

Across the country, church leaders have remarked that the creative ideas we've shared are not only inspiring but also doable. They are relieved to finally find a resource that caters to small or medium-sized churches with limited resources. In fact, a comment we hear often is "I attended a seminar that was given by a mega-church. While I was there I felt inspired—elated. How wouldn't I? The concepts they presented were phenomenal. But when I was back in my own church setting, reality hit hard. There was absolutely no way I could begin to implement the things they'd talked about. We're a small church—growing, but small. After returning home I felt deflated, alone, and discouraged—like no one really understood the limitations I have to work with."

Well, we do understand and we can certainly empathize. We've walked in your shoes. And although you may feel alone at times, realize that this book is written with you in mind. In fact, in order to best develop a tool that applies to the largest variety of churches, all of the Mood Settters and Sermon Boosters ideas were brainstormed by 21 different focus groups. Each group contained people just like you: pastors, worship leaders, lay leaders, drama directors, program team members, actors, technical support staff, etc. These concepts were inspired and conceptualized by others who have the same restrictions as you. We think you'll agree that the ideas in this second volume of *Unforgettable Sundays* are not only valuable and inspiring but also very doable!

Our prayer is that in your quest to promote effective communication, *Unforgettable Sundays Volume Two* will prove to be an invaluable resource. May it stimulate your ideas, be an inspiration and encouragement, help you develop a healthy, proficient programming team, and lighten your workload. After implementing the concepts from this book, we hope that when someone from your congregation is asked "How was church on Sunday?" the response will be an enthusiastic, "Unforgettable!"

Glossary

Term	Definition
Action Step	A practical opportunity for the congregation to put the teachings of the message into action.
Application	A hands-on teaching moment where the pastor or church leader asks people to apply what they've learned.
Building & Grounds	Creative displays or activities outside the building to grab people's attention as they enter the grounds or facility.
Discussion Groups	The congregation divides into small groups to talk about a suggested question or topic.
Drama	Live performances by actors which illustrate the theme of the service. May include a variety of forms such as reader's theater, choral Scripture readings, monologues, slice of life, and situation comedies.
Dress	A specific wardrobe or costume worn by the speaker to enhance the message.
Environment	A setting on the platform that complements the speaker's message, such as a living room or a café.
Greeters	Friendly members positioned near the entrance to welcome people to the service.
Interruption	A planned interjection during the message, used to clarify a point.
Interview	A conversation, where one person asks another questions about a topic, life experience, or opinion that relate to the theme of the service.
Introduction	Short, attention-grabbing moments that set up the theme for the day—a story, anecdote, interview, or reference to current events. The introduction usually is not longer than five minutes in length—it is not a mini-sermon.
Message	The sermon.

Mood Setter	Elements in the service, other than those in the sermon, designed to prepare the congregation for the message.
Object Lesson	A lesson in which the speaker illustrates a point through the use of tangible objects.
Open Mike	A time when the congregation is given the opportunity to share thoughts on a suggested topic, such as "I saw God at work in my life this week when . . ."
Panel Discussion	A group of people—facilitated by a moderator—which discusses the topic of the day from personal standpoints.
Performance Art	Dramatic moments that are performed in places other than the platform. This may be interactive, such as clowns in the lobby.
Power Point	A MicroSoft Office Software package used to design presentations for projections or handouts.
Reading	A member of the congregation reads a selection that coordinates with the theme for the day.
Sermon Booster	Techniques used within the sermon to illustrate a point or to help bring focus to a topic.
Tableau	A form of drama in which actors freeze in a "snapshot" to express a biblical story.
Thematic Service	A worship service in which the elements are focused toward one central theme.
Transition	Musical interludes that help the service flow from one element to the next. These can be live or prerecorded.
Video	A short scene from a movie or another videotape that relates to the theme.
Visual Art	Artistic displays on or around the platform that illustrate the theme.
Welcome	A time during the service to simply welcome regular attendees and visitors.
Worship Programming Team	A team of people from the congregation that meets regularly to design worship services around a central theme.
WOTS	Word on the Street—a videotaped interview of people in the community responding to a simple question.

CHAPTER ONE

Are Your Sundays Forgettable?

We hope not. And we know you don't want them to be forgettable either! But we also know that pastors and church leaders across the country struggle week after week to effectively communicate with their congregations. It seems like you've just closed the service with the benediction and the band begins playing the prelude for next week's service!

But what's happened in the lives of your congregation the week between that benediction and prelude? They've put in forty or more hours at work, taxied kids to soccer games, attended piano recitals, navigated family conflicts, taken in a movie or two, and kept up with the yardwork. Whew! The hectic pace of living has crowded out the memory of what happened last week at church. Sunday has been forgotten.

In addition, people are encouraged to "compartmentalize" their living. They've been taught that one part of their lives should not affect another part of their lives. For example, the office worker is told that it's company policy to keep work and family responsibilities separate. So how does this "categorizing" affect people's view of the church? Frankly, people unconsciously live as if church is something that pertains only to Sunday and not to the rest of the week. It's as if they think, "Sure, on Sundays, I dress up, go to church, smile a lot, and try to look spiritual. But hey, the rest of the week, I'm out in the real world! I'm not sure how my Sunday personality really applies there." As a result, they are discouraged from applying what they learned on Sundays to their daily lives.

To church leaders, this type of attitude is a concern. We find ourselves asking, "How do I help my people not only remember but also apply what they've learned so that lives can be changed?" After all, that's the bottom line for us. But can a one-hour Sunday morning service actually be such an unforgettable experience that people go home and continue growing in their relationship with Christ? Are there ways to use Sundays to teach others to see and respond to the spiritual in all aspects of life? Our answer is a wholehearted yes! In fact, that's exactly what most people in your congregation are longing to encounter. A friend of ours who is a young businessman clarified the desire of many when he shared, "Work is what I do, not who I am. Shouldn't church be who I am, not just something I do?"

Yes, it should be. Our desire is to help you create that kind of experience for your people. Imagine what a difference it would make if the majority of your congregation attended church not just out of habit, but with an attitude of great expectancy. Wouldn't that be phenomenal? That's just one of the many benefits you'll see that will result from creating Unforgettable Sundays.

But I'm Not an Entertainer!

What specifically causes a Sunday service to be unforgettable? Well, there are numerous factors that help congregations remember what was taught on the previous Sunday. Undoubtedly, one of the dilemmas that the church faces today is the fact that it's difficult to compete with the communication methods of our culture. Like it or not, people are used to being entertained by productions that have multimillion dollar budgets. The competition is pretty steep out there! Think about it: radio, sitcoms, movies, Broadway theatre, magazines, MTV, ESPN, CNN, and the Internet—all are greatly influential in the lives of your people. Amazingly, the average adult watches a whopping 36 hours of television a week! Whether you agree with the messages the media is sending is not the issue. The point is, technology is capturing the attention of church people, mostly through entertainment.

"Come on," you say. "That's the job of media—to entertain. Don't go trying to convince me that's the role of the church!" Obviously, it's not. But, stick with us here. There's a big difference between simply amusing your congregation and using some of the methods of technology (or entertainment) to catch the attention of your congregation appropriately and to create meaning. Amusement allows your people to mindlessly idle their time away; it panders to the narcissism that is all too rampant in our culture. But employing creative techniques, some in the classic forms of entertainment, can be purposeful. It's a way to capture interest, keep church attenders focused, and ultimately create meaning that can change lives.

Christian storyteller and comedian Mark Lowry put it this way, "People always ask, is it entertainment or ministry? It better be both. If you don't get their attention, you're not going to be able to minister to them."

Entertainment for entertainment's sake may ultimately be a dead-end trap, just as creativity for creativity's sake can derail worship planners from the significant purpose of upholding Christ and giving forth scriptural truth. Instead, we must learn to use entertainment tools and our God-given creativity to find meaning that celebrates Christ.

So how do we do just that? How do we capture people's attention while simultaneously ministering? Part of the answer is to incorporate creativity into your worship planning. Now for some, just mentioning "getting creative" causes stomachs to do nervous flip-flops. Still, when it comes to designing worship services, you know that something needs to change and it needs to change now! Otherwise you wouldn't be reading this book, right?

When we refer to adding a touch of creativity to your Sunday services, we are by no means suggesting you design a dog and pony show. Hardly! Never would we ask you to compromise your own integrity regarding the sacred work of your people in worship. We're simply suggesting that you strive to find ways to incorporate creative elements into your services in order to help lead your people in fresh, exciting, life-changing Sundays.

By combining visual media, music, drama, and preaching that communicates, you're bringing together a powerful mix to accomplish the important task of making Unforgettable Sundays. And you have enhanced the teaching of spiritual concepts with some of the forms of entertainment that our sight and sound culture employs.

"All right," you say. "I understand what you are talking about, but when I hear the word entertainment, it sends up red flags. Aren't you compromising worship by choosing to also entertain?"

Again, we are using some of the forms and technologies of entertainment to create spiritual meaning. We are not entertaining for the sake of entertaining. However, we are glad you asked the question.

A Trip Backward (and Forward) in Time

Let's take an overview of how God related to humankind over the centuries. Step into our time machine along with Doctor Emmett Brown from the film, *Back to the Future*. Zoom! Bing! Bang! Back we've flown, more than 2,000 years into the days of the Old Testament. Listen. Do you hear the trumpets blowing at the close of the Day of Atonement? Taste the unleavened bread of the Passover. Smell the God-pleasing aroma of the burnt offerings. Hear the crash of the tambourines, the voices lifted in song, the stomping of the dancing feet. See the smiles of the children as they joyfully give presents of food to one another and gifts to the poor.

All these sights, sounds, tastes, smells—these emotionally evocative and tactile elements—are Old Testament worship Mood Setters! In one sense, they could also be considered entertainment—although certainly entertainment with spiritual meaning. These occasions of joy and thanksgiving were purposefully placed by God into the Jewish calendar. All of the senses were used so the worshipers could fully enter into communion with God.

These "moment makers" enhanced Old Testament worship. They uniquely grabbed the Israelites' attention away from the work in the fields and the care of the animals to focus on Jehovah God himself. Even back then, multisensory worship took place so that people could fully enter into communion with God. The tabernacle and temple were filled with symbolism so people could worship him with understanding and meaning. And after the Sabbath, when these worshippers returned home and saw a lamb, you can be sure they remembered the one they saw sacrificed to God at the temple.

Buckle up! We're headed for Israel in the year A.D. 31. Zoom! Zap! Bing! All right, everybody out. We're at the Sea of Galilee. Look there on the water. It's Jesus—preaching from a fishing boat. He's telling stories of the kingdom! Notice the people in the crowd. They're enraptured as he weaves spiritual truths into his storytelling, stories about things they encounter every day: a sower and his seeds, worthless weeds and mustard seeds, yeast and pearls and fish.

Jesus, an extraordinary communicator, is using Sermon Boosters. He encourages personal interaction by asking questions of his listeners. As people press him with questions, he's not afraid of interruptions. Instead, he responds to the environment around him by telling stories with familiar places, objects, and characters. He's adaptable; he moves to a boat in the water when the crowd gets too big. As he talks, people are challenged not just to listen but also to respond. Those who truly open their hearts are forever changed.

Back into our time machine. Ting! Bang! Boom! Yikes, the flux capacitor must be stuck! We're traveling swiftly now. Time is fast-forwarding over the video screen. Hey, we're arriving at a church in the Middle Ages! Looks like they're also speaking the language of their culture. Good thing, because in those days, people were illiterate. The printed word of Scripture is being taught through the visual word—mosaics, paintings, stained glass, and sculptures. And what's that big cartlike thing in front of the church? Oh, it looks like church drama has moved from the sanctuary to the street.

Hold on! This crazy time-traveling contraption is taking off again! This time we're inside a 21st century church. Let's check it out.

Notice the large banner that reads "Press On" hanging over the entrance to the church. The greeters are dressed in running uniforms and wearing those paper race numbers; they sure are friendly. The worship band sounds great. Everyone's singing enthusiastically. On to the sermon. What's this? The pastor is interviewing the Apostle Paul. "Paul, what advice can you give this church in the 21st century?"

"This one thing," Paul responds. "Press on toward the goal to win the prize for which God has called you heavenward. Press on!"

Our plutonium is getting low; it's time we head for home. Bing! Azp! Zzzwweee! What a trip! Whoops, sorry about your hair. We forgot to roll up the windows before that last takeoff.

Perhaps you can see that the ideas we are presenting aren't new. They're just translations of cultural meaning in the same way the Scriptures have been translated into languages people can understand. It's not new to use art—it's just that the art of our contemporary culture is different, more media-oriented, more technologically enhanced.

Obviously, during Jesus' time, there were artists, poets, musicians, and storytellers. Christ preached in a time that placed high value on the oral tradition; it was not a print-dominated culture. In a sense, Christ preached to a sight and sound generation. In the same way today, meaningful worship elements can grab the attention of your congregation and focus it on the theme of the sermon. Technology and the arts are coming together as communication tools capable of creating life-changing worship services in our modern sight and sound culture. Technology has become the campfire around which we tell our stories.

Not long ago, the founding pastor of our church celebrated his hundredth birthday. We didn't know he was going to attend the service one morning—a service that began with an edgy, upbeat tune. After the song, Pastor Newell struggled to the platform. Unable to make it up the steps, he sat on the edge of the stage holding a microphone. "This generation," he began, "doesn't do things the way mine did." We all held our breath, acutely aware of the volume and beat of the preceding special music. "But, dearly beloved, that has never bothered me," he continued. "You see, God has worked differently down through the ages, and when I see things being done differently today than in my generation, it is evidence that he's still alive and moving."

Fortunately, the church today is beginning to do things differently. We are changing. We're beginning to realize that the thinking that brought us where we are today won't launch us into the future. After all, who would have believed that many mainstream churches of every denomination would no longer solely use hymnals or the majestic sounds of a pipe organ?

If the church is failing to reach people now, is it because we are not doing what Jesus did? He spoke the language of his culture out of a desire to make the Father known. And that must be our motivation, too. The Apostle Paul understood it when he said, "I have become all things to all men so that by all possible means I might save some" (1 Corinthians 9:22). People outside the church whom we are trying to reach often think of the church as archaic, irrelevant, and boring. They may not be far from wrong if, instead of doing as Jesus did, we refuse to speak truth appropriately using the media and technological language of our culture. Recently, we heard someone define insanity as "doing things the same way and expecting different results." Makes sense to us. How about you?

Creativity Is for Churches of All Sizes

"Okay, you guys. I agree with what you're saying. But obviously you haven't been to my church. We have a small congregation of under a hundred people. Our hands are tied. Our resources are limited."

Well, here's some good news. Maybe we haven't been to your specific church, but please understand, we've consulted with and taught in similar churches across the country. In fact, we wrote this book with you in mind. It's a misconception that a church has to be large, with tons of funding, in order to create unforgettable Sunday experiences. As you read on, you'll soon realize that most of the ideas in the matrix of this book can be done on a small budget in a small church. Isn't that refreshing? Authors who attend mega-churches with unlimited resources didn't write this book. Believe us, we more than understand the process of trying to be creative in the midst of budget cuts, necessary scrimping, begging, and borrowing! So read on and we'll further explain what makes a Sunday service memorable.

Specifically, what are Unforgettable Sundays? Well, they're Sundays that help staff and lay people alike experience the living reality of Christ, our Lord and Savior. It's as though Jesus is physically present among us and we can see, touch, hear, and respond to him in ways that alter our lives forever. "We have seen the Lord!" should not only be the amazed exclamation of the disciples who witnessed his Resurrection long ago. Rather, it should be the cry of every Christian heart, every Sunday.

Unforgettable Sundays, week after week, year after year, help us to restore the inward vision, the eyes of the soul. In our present day, we long to shout that ancient witness of all the disciples: "He is here! Christ is risen! The Lord is alive!" Week after week, Unforgettable Sundays help us celebrate Jesus. They enable us to discover and rediscover what makes him so very attractive to so many.

Have you ever experienced an Unforgettable Sunday? Try to recall at least one Sunday church experience that made a difference in the rest of your life. Does something come to mind? Perhaps it took place years ago, but you still remember the preacher's theme and sermon points. Maybe a missionary gave such a remarkable report from the field that you were challenged to Christian service. Or possibly, through watching a powerful drama, a deep desire to be more godly was ignited. Since that time you've experienced surprising spiritual growth.

Now ask yourself: Is it possible to make Sundays unforgettable? What do you think? Can we really expect church goers' lives to be significantly impacted fifty-two weeks a year, year after year? This book is dedicated to helping you do just that. We believe, through the guidance of the Holy Spirit, you too can create Unforgettable Sundays that impact your congregation in life-changing ways, week after week. When preplanning your worship services, you'll immediately recognize the central role that Scripture takes. In fact, for us, that's always where our brainstorming sessions begin—with the pastor's preaching topic, with the Scripture text, and with a great dependence on the work of prayer throughout the entire creating process.

Wait! Where's the Holy Spirit?

"Okay, obviously the idea of creating Unforgettable Sundays is highly appealing. But doesn't all the brainstorming and the preplanning of the worship services hinder the spontaneous work of the Holy Spirit?"

Certainly, worship leaders must be sensitive to those remarkable moments that are given birth despite the most well-laid plans. How often have ministers, at the last minute, abandoned their prepared sermons for the sake of a personal testimony that deeply touched the hearts of the hearers? Frequently, prayers for healing give rise to congregational intercession with dramatic results in the souls of all gathered. Think about how often we hear of some weeping sinner spontaneously confessing his or her sins. Because of this unplanned moment, the opportunity then rises for a powerful work of God among the rest of the congregation.

Flexibility and sensitivity to the moment are important. Worship leaders—lay people and staff—must learn to watch for the ways God moves among us despite our previous intentions. On the other hand, to think that the Holy Spirit can't work weeks ahead as we preplan services is to hold to an extremely limited view of his amazing abilities! Prophets, moved by the Word of the Lord, foretold the coming of the Messiah centuries before the actual event. God, time and again in the Scriptures, gave promises that would be fulfilled decades after the initial pronouncements. Can we possibly think we humans will limit his omniscience by our small agendas and our minuscule attempts at preplanning?

How many times have circumstances similar to the following occurred? A worship team works several weeks in advance to plan a service around the central theme of God's comfort. The week before that very preplanned Sunday, a person in the congregation is killed in a tragic automobile accident. Through the shock, the grief, and the dismay, a whole church is nevertheless reminded that God enfolds us with his unending love and mercy, even in the midst of terror and tragedy. That's an Unforgettable Sunday.

Planning teams frequently find themselves giving testimony to the preknowledge of the Holy Spirit. "We didn't know," they will tell one another, "but God sure knew what we would be facing on that day and what we would need to remember about him." Worship preplanning more frequently evidences God's sovereignty in our small human affairs than it offends the spontaneous work of the Holy Spirit. Our suggestion: Try worship preplanning and be frequently amazed at the way God works way ahead of all our best efforts.

The Resources Right Under Your Nose

This workbook is designed to help you plan Sundays that celebrate Jesus in life-changing worship. There are two principles we teach that will help transform unremarkable Sundays into unforgettable ones. The first principle is to form worship programming teams that are comprised of both lay people and staff. This team begins to bear the responsibility for brainstorming, designing, and executing your worship services. The second principle is to theme each worship service around one main spiritual concept or one key biblical truth.

Now then, what's so important about establishing a programming team? The answer to that question is simple: Everything! Next to the preacher's own Bible study, the whispers of the Holy Spirit in sermon preparation, and those shelves of commentaries, lay people are one of the greatest and most underutilized worship resources.

Why are they so important? Very simply, those people looking up at the preacher from the pews Sunday after Sunday are the very Body of Christ. They are the church—these men, women, youth, and children. To refrain from drawing upon them as a key resource in worship planning is neglect, to say the least, if not outright professional clergy arrogance, to say the worst.

Invite them to participate in a worship programming team. Establish a core value of discovering and using the spiritual gifts of the laity. There are artists and technicians of all kinds who are longing to share their skills. Build a programming team made up of all sorts of creative people from your church. Find a leader with a passion to create life-changing worship services in a sight and sound culture. Add to the mix an audio technician, a Scripture whiz, an avid reader, and a scribe to keep track of everything. Throw in an all-around creative consultant (those people with way-out ideas and "why not" attitudes), find a good administrator, and you've got yourself a team! Be sure to also keep an empty chair at the planning table to help the team remember that Jesus, through the Holy Spirit, is in the planning process as well as in the Sunday service.

Now what happens? Suddenly the work of fifty-two Sundays, year after year, decade after decade, is distributed upon the shoulders of people whose creativity is seemingly unlimited, whose eagerness to do worship with excellence seems unbounded. These are the people whose feet and hands are in the marketplace, who can give feedback as to whether the sermon theme is hitting the mark anywhere near their everyday lives. Moms and dads will have endless ideas for children's sermons. Lay artists will do whatever it takes to integrate expressive forms into the worship time—dance, drama, painting, or fabrics turned into glorious panels.

The lives of lay people become the very stuff out of which engaging sermon illustrations are birthed. Freely, joyfully, they'll give you the impacting story, the poignant life-moment, the perfect idea for congregational response, an incident from a popular book everyone is reading (except you), a movie concept, the exact statistics, etc. Lay people are a living pool of abounding and unending resources. A group of lay people will help you plan worship so that all the learning styles in the congregation are challenged. Given half a chance, they are endlessly original, grateful simply to be respected and used, often surprisingly culturally relevant, wise, and vulnerable.

Why would any pastor or any staff not utilize their lay people in a worship programming team? As far as we can see, this latent, powerful resource far outweighs any negatives. Interestingly enough, the matrix included in this Unforgettable Sundays, Volume II was brainstormed by twenty-one focus groups including lay people, worship planning teams, and pastors from multiple denominations and nondenominational churches. The matrix is proof itself of the unlimited resources available through this programming principle: Form worship programming teams that are comprised of both lay people and staff. For further help and information in building a dynamic worship planning team and how it should work, see *Unforgettable Sundays, volume one*, chapter three.

Tie It All Together

The second principle is the practice of planning the service around one central theme, one organizing metaphor, or one key biblical truth. In a sense, the whole service is the sermon. The praise and worship music, the call to worship, the announcements, the offering, the drama, the response or invitation, all can enhance the chosen Sunday morning theme. Though the sermon is the fulcrum around which all these ingredients make a compatible whole, the different elements of the service amplify and extend, illustrate or foreshadow, the central meaning of the morning through a variety of approaches that keep attention and create meaning.

This is essential in a culture overwhelmed with information. We're bombarded with messages trying to get us to do this, do that, go here, try something, buy something, learn, absorb, understand, integrate, join, participate, protest, attend, refrain, refuse, excuse, and defend. What a relief to come together in worship and have the time to focus our minds and hearts on one main theme that helps us praise and celebrate the living presence of Christ.

Often Sundays are forgettable because they consist of fragmented pieces that do not build on each other, do not enhance the sermon, and provide no central life-changing idea that lay people can grasp. One central organizing concept allows the mind and heart to focus on meaning. People will learn through repetition and through various learning styles that reiterate the same main theme. All parts of the service—from the announcements to the sermon—can be coordinated to emphasize this one basic idea. Again, the whole service becomes the sermon. Sight, sound, touch, taste, and feel—all senses are engaged in spiritual learning. Sundays become life-changing and unforgettable by incorporating just a few meaningful shifts at a time.

This thematic approach also allows the worship programming team to work ahead, even when the pastor's sermon is not totally fleshed out. All a team needs is the main scriptural passage and a key sentence explaining where the pastor is going with his sermon. With this much information, a programming team can begin to brainstorm creative elements that will support and enhance the worship service.

Two planning principles will help make Sundays unforgettable: (1) Forming a worship programming team, and (2) Organizing the service around one theme. We strongly suggest that you attempt to make them core principles in your worship planning.

What They Want

Perhaps you would like to know what other elements our focus groups felt were necessary in making Sundays unforgettable. Sundays are unforgettable if we:

- Include an element of surprise.
- Thematically plan the service to relate to the sermon.
- Clearly present practical, hands-on applications that people can take with them through the week and use to change their lives.
- Do things with excellence (or at least the best that we can do) and establish this value of excellence in ministry by planning in advance.
- Relate to different learning styles.
- Translate spiritual content appropriately using the language of our culture.
- Build a programming team that relies on the Holy Spirit for guidance in creativity and is free to tap into the creative resources around us; this establishes a core value of discovering and using lay gifts.
- Work to make church the highlight of the week.
- Build a safe environment that encourages risk-taking and creativity.
- Challenge the status quo like Jesus did within the boundaries of biblical Christian faith.
- Employ the arts as communication tools.
- Week after week, acknowledge the presence of Jesus in the planning process as well as in the Sunday service.

And please remember: You don't have to do everything on a grand scale. Just do what you can and do it well. Sometimes simple is extremely profound. Congregation members may not like new ways of doing things in your services only because you didn't take the time to do them the best you could with the resources available. Establish the value of excellence in ministry by planning your services far enough in advance. We recommend four to six weeks. (Okay. You can get up off the floor now!) Really, four to six weeks advance planning is not that hard to do once you get into the routine. This gives your team enough time to pull resources together, build, write, and rehearse. It's when we scramble to pull together a service at the last minute that it ends up feeling shoddy or disconnected. No wonder people react negatively to "new" ideas. It's amazing what can be done with the proper time and planning and how receptive congregations can be to prayerful, appropriate, and meaningful change.

When worship is restored, great joy visits God's people. May we be like those who saw the restoration during Nehemiah's day. "The two choirs that gave thanks then took their places in the house of God. . . . On that day they offered great sacrifices, rejoicing because God had given them great joy. The women and children also rejoiced. The sound of rejoicing in Jerusalem could be heard far away" (Nehemiah 12:40, 43).

May we know again, in our land, the joy of Unforgettable Sundays.

CHAPTER TWO

How Can We Make
Sundays Unforgettable?

Unforgettable Sundays: volume two (the sequel to *Unforgettable Sundays: volume one*) is here with more Mood Setters and more Sermon Boosters to help create life-changing worship services in a sight and sound culture. We've chosen and brainstormed eight broad themes that are easily preachable—such as prayer, humility, encouragement, truth, and so forth.

Under each broad theme, you'll find three Scripture passages that relate to the section's overall concept. Here's where this resource becomes a huge time-saver for you. Each Scripture passage then has between twenty to thirty cutting-edge ideas to choose from and incorporate into your own worship planning.

You'll also find a listing of related topics, allowing this book to be used as an extensive resource that applies to a wide range of Christian themes other than the specific ones we've chosen. That's more than six months of Sunday planning with enough creative ideas to carry you ten years and beyond. We call these creative ideas Mood Setters and Sermon Boosters.

If you've used *Unforgettable Sundays: volume one*, then you already know that all Mood Setters and Sermon Boosters focus on enhancing those things we already do in church. We're not talking about reinventing the wheel. Adding a little creativity doesn't require changing your whole service so your congregation ends up wondering, "Hey, did a different church move into this building when I wasn't looking?" We're simply giving you ideas that can help you serve your congregation. Each one is designed to creatively point to the sermon topic for the day.

If your church is participating in the 50-Day Spiritual Adventure titled "Celebrate Jesus," utilizing this book will be a snap. Each of the eight weekly Spiritual Adventure themes correlates to the eight overall themes in *Unforgettable Sundays: volume two*. In each of these chapters, you will also find three of the recommended Scripture passages that coincide with the 50-Day Adventure, "Celebrate Jesus." But participating in that specific spiritual adventure isn't necessary to gain benefit from these helps. They are designed to stand on their own.

To make things easier, we've categorized all the creative ideas under general themes. And, to benefit you even further, we've designed and included eight sample thematic worship services that are included as the last theme at the end of each matrix chapter.

If you're just beginning to incorporate creative elements into your planning, you may find you'll only want to pull one idea from each sample service. In fact, we strongly recommend that you not go fast with changes. Give the Holy Spirit time to work the meaning of these elements into the hearts of your congregation.

Now, to simplify things even more, we've divided all the creative ideas into two separate categories—Mood Setters and Sermon Boosters.

Are you still with us? Here's a quick review: (1) Eight overall themes divided further into three more related topics with coordinated Scripture passages. (2) One fully planned worship service per theme. (3) All brainstorm ideas divided into two categories: Mood Setters and Sermon Boosters.

"The Big Game"

When it comes to the Super Bowl, "the game" is the thing. Without the game, all we have is weeks of meaningless commentary and professional speculation. (Even with the game there's lots of that!) When the final two teams have won the right to contend for this monumental honor, the media hoopla cranks up the heat and for the next two weeks all we hear about is the Super Bowl.

Whether it's the morning traffic reporter or the small town paper, everyone has an insight and opinion on the final outcome of the game. Without the game there would be no Super Bowl. But the same tends to hold true in reverse. Without the pre- and postgame media blitz, there would be no real Super Bowl experience either. Imagine if the next Super Bowl isn't covered on the news or in the papers. The only time it is mentioned is on the actual game day, just five minutes before the opening kickoff. The point is, without the pregame and postgame coverage, the Super Bowl would be just one more football game.

The same can be said about your sermons. When your people arrive for church on Sunday morning, their minds are still scattered across an entire week of activities. Not to mention the panic that took place that very morning just trying to get to church on time. Your people need help to slow down, refocus, tune in, and get in touch with their heavenly Father. The Lord says, "Be still, and know that I am God" (Psalm 46:10). This verse isn't only speaking of quieting your tongue, but also your mind. "Be still," God tells us. "Listen to my voice and *only* my voice. Take time to turn off the other areas of your life that are constantly bombarding you for attention."

Let's think of Sunday mornings as "the big game." This upcoming sermon is like the Super Bowl of the week. Are your people ready? Have you helped them get excited about the big plays God is designing? Have you practiced your colorful commentating so you'll be sure to paint an accurate and dynamic picture as the game unfolds? Are lay people eagerly anticipating a sermon that they'll talk about for weeks to come? Have you planned to follow up the big event with a figurative postgame interview, analysis of the major plays, and helpful commentary that brings the whole sermon into perspective?

The Super Bowl is the Super Bowl because of what happens before, during, and after the event. The same is true for your sermons. How you prepare your people to hear God's Word will have a great impact on whether this is an Unforgettable Sunday, or one that fades into a long season of similar forgotten sermons. Through the use of what we call Mood Setters and Sermon Boosters, we'll help you design Sunday mornings that captivate your people rather than allow them to be passive observers.

Mood Setters are creative techniques that help people focus on the theme of the service. They take place before and after your sermon: They're like the pregame analysis that allows people to understand the topic of the day and focus on the sermon that's coming up; they are also like post-game highlights that help people assimilate the sermon points into their lives.

Sermon Boosters are like the colorful commentary that brings the sermon alive, captures the congregation's attention, and gives them tangible reminders to hold onto for weeks, months, and even years to come. Just as Super Bowls can be remembered as unforgettable games, Sunday morning services that incorporate Mood Setters and Sermon Boosters can take on legendary, and even more importantly, life-changing characteristics for your people. Let us explain how.

Mood Setters

Take a look at two different restaurants. Walk through the door of the first and you're immediately hit with the aroma of fried chicken that permeates the establishment. The restaurant is lit with fluorescent lights. You walk up to a red Formica counter and are greeted by a person wearing a red and white checked paper hat. You place your order. It's called out over a microphone. You pay the person behind the counter and receive a paper bag filled with your dinner. What kind of dining experience have you just had? Fast food? Precisely.

Now let's visit another restaurant. You walk through the door and immediately notice that the lights are dimmed. Soft, romantic music is playing in the background. A maître d' with a

French accent greets you and politely escorts you to your reserved table for two. Soft light from a single candle illuminates a fresh rose that is displayed in a crystal vase upon the neatly pressed linen tablecloth. As you take your seat, a violinist strolls by and stops to play at your table. What kind of restaurant are you in now?

As we travel across the country and pose this question to the attendees at our conferences, an interesting thing always happens. Typically, the men answer, "Expensive." But the women usually respond, "Romantic." Or the ladies might also tease, "Sounds like some place I've never been, but would love to go to!"

Regardless, each of these restaurants has its own unique mood that cued you into what kind of dining experience was ahead. In each, elements such as lighting, smells, music, greeters, uniforms, and so forth helped to establish a particular mood. You didn't stroll into the fast food restaurant and expect to find a maître d' or soft lighting. Establishing a mood allows patrons of individual restaurants to know what to expect when dining.

The same is true when attending a church service. Lighting, visuals, music, greeters, scents, and sounds are all experienced when someone walks through the doors of your church. They create a specific atmosphere or mood. So how is a specific mood established that heightens a person's worship experience? The answer is by utilizing what we call Mood Setters.

Mood Setters are unique ways of grabbing people's attention and focusing it on the theme of the service. These are extremely important because they often contain the element of surprise, like a teacher clapping her hands and saying, "Now students. Pay attention!" These "moment makers" enhance the worship service and can take place at any time during a worship service except the sermon. Here's a sample list of areas that could be enhanced by using Mood Setters:

Announcements—How do you make this time complement the theme of the day? It's not difficult. Just add a little creativity and let your imagination run wild. You could have two people dialogue the announcements if the theme of the day is on friendships. Add an unexpected element every now and then. Have fun!

If the service is on evangelism and the sermon title is "Stop Striking Out When You Witness," a staff person could dress up like a hotdog vendor at a sporting event and give the announcements by calling them out in that singsong vendor style. Maybe your church is starting a new series called, "Bought and Paid for by Christ." One way to deliver the announcements thematically is to have someone act as a store clerk. Have others walk onto the platform holding shopping baskets or even pushing a few shopping carts. One by one they could say something like, "Excuse me, could you tell me where to find the women's morning prayer breakfast?" "Yes, ma'am, you'll find it coming this Saturday at 9 a.m. sharp in the Fellowship Hall. They're having a special if you bring a friend—two for the price of one. You'll find a coupon for it in your bulletin."

The key is to not get into the same old rut. Consider projecting the announcements onto a screen behind the platform or creating a video piece. How about even using a puppet to give your announcements? Better yet, is there someone who could make a puppet "look alike" of your pastor? Get the idea? The main purpose is to grab the congregation's attention, get the announcements out, and if possible, also help direct them toward the theme of the day.

Building and Grounds—First impressions are important, even when made from a distance. As people drive up to your church on Sunday morning, the first thing they see is the building and grounds. How do they look? Are they well-maintained? What impressions do they make? Newcomers will often make a decision to return or not based on their "feelings" during the first ten minutes of their visit. Think about it— you've got ten minutes! That's hardly enough time for people to park the car, unload, and enter the sanctuary! How can you make a positive impression even before the congregation has the chance to get seated? Use the church's building and grounds to help.

Setting up the sermon through creative Mood Setters can be used even from the moment someone pulls into the parking lot and walks up to the church doors. Consider using visual cues that help people focus on the sermon topic. For example, a large banner waving in the wind to announce a new sermon series will draw attention and signal that something exciting is happening. Or use something even more eye-catching. If the sermon topic is "The Kingship of Christ," help illustrate that point by having a red carpet rolled down the sidewalk toward the entrance to the sanctuary.

Want another idea? Let's say today's sermon is titled, "Living the Balanced Christian Life." How could you get people thinking about that theme even before they enter the sanctuary? Dress a drama person from your congregation in a traditional mime costume complete with face paint. As people walk into your church's front entrance, have the actor pantomime trying to keep balanced while walking an imaginary tight rope on the sidewalk. Now that would grab people's attention! Before your congregation even sets foot through the doors, you've communicated something. Already they're engaged in the service and want to find out more. Take advantage of that curiosity. At the beginning of the service, have someone explain how what was happening outside the sanctuary ties in with the theme of the service or the sermon topic—a minimal amount of effort that allows you to quickly focus people's hearts and minds!

Communion—One of the most powerful and simple examples we've used as a Communion Mood Setter involved a basic nail. When the congregation came forward to receive the elements, a simple carpenter's nail was gently placed in each of their hands. When they returned to their seats, they took the nail with them as a way of remembering that Jesus suffered on the cross for their sins. What a powerful and eye-opening effect it had on our people! Some people carried that nail in their pockets for years. We know because they showed us. Keeping your communion moments simple is important, but keeping your communion time effective and life-changing is just as important.

Greeters and Ushers—Sports coat and tie. Floral dress and pumps. Sound like the attire your greeters and ushers usually wear? Certainly you want them to be nicely dressed, friendly people. That's understandable. But, why not, when appropriate, also utilize these service teams to accent the day's theme? For instance, if the message is called, "Resuscitating Your Spiritual Life," consider having them wear something that hints at what the message is about. You could drape stethoscopes around their necks. Or if you really want to go all out, dress them in complete doctor's scrubs. Once your congregation is greeted and seated by someone dressed this way, from that point on, they'll be looking for clues as to how these visuals tie in with the sermon.

A word about appropriateness. Often churches establish a contemporary service and a traditional service because what is appropriate, helpful, and thought-provoking for some is a hindrance for others. If you're planning a service for a congregation with a mix of both styles then exercise compassionate wisdom. Be willing to struggle with appropriateness for the sake of all concerned. Prayerfully consider what you can introduce and the Holy Spirit will teach and guide you as to what is the correct and sensitive approach for change.

Introduction—Can you picture a simple dollhouse? There it sits—right on a pedestal next to the pulpit. It's been there since the beginning of the worship service, yet no one's mentioned anything about it. Not a word. Does the pastor even see it? Certainly the minister of music must have noticed. So why is it there? Everyone's curious.

A simple visual can have quite the impact, can't it? The introduction time begins by someone picking up the dollhouse cue and explaining, "Today we're starting a new series on family relationships. As we begin today, let this dollhouse be a reminder to evaluate how you're doing at making your family a priority."

Sure, you could have easily said all of that without the use of a prop. But how many would have really listened to you? Would they have remembered what the focus of the new series was a half hour after church? Introducing a new series or the sermon topic is always enhanced by attaching it to the minds of your people with some visual symbol. Piles of stones in the wilderness were memorial markers of God's work among his people. Don't be afraid to use visuals as symbolic memorials.

Lighting—Remember our previous restaurant examples? Lighting plays a big part in helping to create a mood. That's true whether you're dining out or entering the sanctuary on Sunday morning. If your service theme is "Celebrating New Life Found in Christ," you probably don't want the sanctuary lights dimmed the entire time. You may decide to start out that way to symbolize the fact that before we know Christ we are entirely lost. But once your emphasis is on accepting Jesus as your personal Savior, you'll undoubtedly want to flood the sanctuary with light. You may even think about renting some special lighting in order to create a celebration type atmosphere with colored lights or spotlights. Lighting is one Mood Setter category that is often forgotten or overlooked. Don't forget the importance of considering how lighting can truly enhance and develop a mood for your service.

Offering—This is a time of reflection and giving back to the Lord for all he's done. For many, it is an act of worship. How can the offering time become a section that also communicates thematically? A simple way to accomplish this is to substitute the offering basket or plate with something that symbolizes the service's theme. If the sermon is titled "The Lord of the Harvest," why not use a small basket or a galvanized gardener's crate to collect the gifts? The person leading the offering time can explain that these objects were chosen to collect the gifts and are to be visual reminders of the theme of the day. When considering an alternate for the offering plate, be sure that the "surprise" doesn't detract from the service. It's important to keep a sense of reverence and avoid the temptation to become trendy. Watch for the extremes. Ask: Will this enhance or detract? You are searching to use only items that will enhance.

Another idea to utilize during the offering time is to allow people to "personalize" the gifts they're offering to the Lord. For example, if the sermon's main theme is forgiveness, pass out 3 x 5 cards for people to write the name of someone they've made a decision to forgive. When the offering is passed, ask them to also drop in their cards as an "offering of obedience" to God.

Prelude and Postlude—What's the first and last "impression" you want your congregation to experience during that service? The music choices for entering and exiting the sanctuary should be selected to correspond and enhance the theme of the day. Consider the words, as well as the tone of each piece. Be purposeful in the choices you make. Be sure that the prelude and postlude are not just fillers, but Mood Setters that truly strengthen the rest of the service. One pastor of a liturgical church employs a tape with monks singing a Gregorian chant. The soft lighting and this music before the choir processional invite his people into silence and prayer.

For example, if the topic of the day is "Influencing Our World with the Love of Christ," the service could be opened with the children's chorus, "This Little Light of Mine." Play it simply, just a one-finger melody allowing the music to communicate, "I'm timid. I'm really not sure how to let my light shine." At the close of the service, after teaching and encouragement on the topic, let loose with the same song in an upbeat, bold, in-your-face jazz style—something that communicates, "I'm empowered to let my light shine!"

Transitions—The welcome has just finished and the associate pastor walks off the platform. Now the drama team is setting up for their part. Two actors carry on a table and a third is carrying two chairs. What's missing? A transition of some kind—perhaps music that fills in the gaps and awkward dead spaces. Transition music helps keep a flow to your services. It communicates, "There is a plan. We know what we're doing."

If your welcome was bright and cheerful and your drama has the same tone, then your music should also be . . . well, you get the idea, don't you? But what if the welcome was cheerful, but the drama starts more on a serious tone? You'll probably want to rethink the transition music. Either it stays cheerful allowing the drama to have a real surprise punch to it, or the music selection could be a little heavier to set up your drama. The choice is yours.

When transition music is thematically tied to the service, it helps drive the message home. Again, take the song example we used in the Prelude and Postlude section. If you chose the song, "This Little Light of Mine," there would be numerous ways to weave it throughout the service and between the worship elements. You could change the feel or the style of the chorus to keep the service moving. Play it in a minor key to set up a serious reading, or in a very soft, meditative style during communion. Record the children singing it joyfully to set up a video clip. By the time the pastor gets up to give the message, there'll be no doubt what he's going to talk about.

There are many parts to a service. Think about how often people are coming and going from the platform. Transitions, whether they are someone softly playing on the piano, a selection from a worship CD, or some kind of prerecorded sounds, are a tool for blending all the elements of your service. It can truly bind your worship into a much more dynamic, fluid, and united service.

Visual Art—Most likely your church has many skilled artists who are looking for opportunities to use their talents. By involving these individuals in a Visual Arts Ministry, you can bring added life to a worship service.

What falls under the category of visual art? The possibilities are as extensive as the creativity of your artists. Ideas can range from banners to collages to photography—and anywhere in between.

Picture your church lobby. Same as usual, nothing out of the ordinary. Now imagine your lobby with a large collection of portraits artistically mounted and displayed. Generations of engaging family photographs fill the foyer for people to gather around and guess who's who.

Can you feel the excitement? The lobby is buzzing with conversations like, "Oh look there. That's Charlie Fox! I remember him. He used to teach Sunday school when I was a boy." If the message is "God's Faithfulness Throughout the Generations," your congregation has already been equipped to fully focus on that topic. They are eagerly right where you want them to be and the service hasn't even started yet!

Welcome—This necessary, yet sometimes awkward, part of the service can be easily and dynamically blended into the day's theme. If your theme is "Making Family a Priority," try using an outgoing family from your church to deliver the morning welcome. In some places, it would be appropriate to perform a little skit by setting up a breakfast table environment on the platform. This provides a way for the family to extend a welcome while casually drinking coffee and discussing with their kids how the morning theme relates to each of them. A creative solution to your welcome time can bring life to an otherwise ordinary part of the service.

Now, obviously, each of the service elements described above is familiar to you. Most likely they are already part of your worship services. That's one reason Mood Setters are so easy to implement. Simply rethink a few of the things you're already doing. There's no need to add a whole new worship element to your service. What you choose can be—and in some places should be—extremely subtle. All you have to do is pick a couple of unique ways to get people thinking about the sermon topic even before the sermon begins. Spend some time brainstorming creative ways that those categories can be used to enhance the theme of your sermon or service.

Sermon Boosters

We live in a society and culture that is heavily influenced by the media. Our people in the pews are no different. They watch television, surf the web, read the papers, rent videos, and go to movies. How is it the media can capture people's attention and accomplish a very difficult task such as helping them remember the products they're selling? It's because advertisers know that people remember information given to them through visuals and sounds.

Imagine you're at a movie theater. The film is about to begin. As usual, first they show the previews of upcoming attractions. Except today, things are a little different. Instead of projecting the previews onto the screen, a man or woman walks down to the front of the theater, stands behind a podium, and describes the upcoming movies using a lecture format. Well, you can be pretty sure the movie executive responsible for that brilliant change in format will soon be lucky to have a job at the concession stand.

Movie-making empires understand that we live in a sight and sound culture. They know people enjoy watching previews that quickly tap into an emotional response, are highly visual, and are heightened with mood-enhancing music and sound effects. The previews are the best of the best. If it's a romantic movie, a preview will depict lovers who travel halfway across the world to finally reach one another and then ride off into the sunset together.

Fast forward to four months later. While leafing through the entertainment section of the newspaper, an unsuspecting movie-goer comes across an ad for that same romantic movie. "Honey, honey, that movie finally came out! You know, the one where I cried through the entire preview. We have to see it tonight!" Previews *do* work. They imprint a message that lasts for months.

While leading our conferences, we took a poll asking the following questions:

1. How many of you use multimillion dollar special effects on Sunday mornings?

2. How many of you have a stable of professional writers to create your drama scripts, calls to worship, and responsive readings?

3. How many of you use world renowned cinematographers to shoot your video inserts?

The official final tally of our survey is as follows: 0, 0, 0. Zero, Zip, Nada! Hollywood, however, has all of these resources in abundance. What do we have? What we have is the most important message of all time: God loves us and Christ died for us. That message decides the eternal fate of each living human being. Week after week we *must* put everything we have into making sure that we communicate this message to our people. We teach through our sermons so that lives are changed. But what if come Monday, our people can't remember what the sermon was about, let alone how to apply it to their lives?

Well, that's where Sermon Boosters come in. Sermon Boosters are effective ways to help "boost" our sermons so that our congregations will be able retain the points and apply the messages we're preaching.

To reiterate, Sermon Boosters are creative attention-grabbing techniques that take place within the sermon. At our conferences, it's fun to see pastor's and church leader's eyes light up when we present the concept of Sermon Boosters. During a conference we'll usually ask, "What help do you need when it comes to your sermons?" It's not uncommon for some bold soul to comment, "I not only need help keeping people's attention, I need help keeping my people awake!" Can you relate? Our conference attendees sure do. Typically, in response to this honest answer, laughter spreads across the room as heads nod in agreement.

How would you have answered that question? If you're also looking for ways to grab people's attention and keep them focused during your sermon, then you'll probably want to begin incorporating a few Sermon Boosters right away!

Why did we choose the term Sermon Booster? Because to "boost" means to lend a helping hand, to hoist, to offer assistance, to support—all these verbs describe what a Sermon Booster does. There are numerous creative ways to give a sermon a little boost.

Sermon Boosters are also helpful in imprinting the message in your congregation's memory. Why is it that some sermons are remembered for a lifetime while others are almost instantly forgotten? While researching this book, we asked people to recall one sermon that made a huge impact in their lives. Certainly, a few who were surveyed responded by saying, "Golly, I just can't think of any." But those who had been impacted profoundly talked about that experience with great passion and detail! And interestingly, the unforgettable sermons were the ones that used some form of a Sermon Booster.

Below is an extensive list of the Sermon Booster ideas we've designed. As you read through the brief descriptions, note which ones appeal most to you. These will be booster ideas you probably should try first. It's best to begin with ones that feel the most comfortable, and as time goes, try those that sound a little more daring.

Action Steps—There are two kinds of action steps that will be referred to in this book— one deals with a preproduced video segment and the second refers to hands-on exercises or assignments that you give your people to do.

"Video Action Steps," produced by Mainstay Church Resources, are creative, fast-paced vignettes that entertain, while at the same time communicate practical assignments to be completed over the next week or so. Video Action Steps are usually three to five minutes in length and focus on a variety of different themes.

Hands-on action steps are assignments that your congregation participates in typically during or just after the service. For example, if the sermon is titled, "Getting Rid of Sin in Your Life," a garbage can may be placed at the exit of the sanctuary. As a practical application to the service, people are invited to discard a piece of paper with the name of a specific troubling sin written on it into this garbage can as they leave.

These action steps are usually simple in nature, but can have a powerful impact because they immediately involve your people by inviting them to take action. Both kinds of Action Steps are usually easy to incorporate and are deeply appreciated by sincere believers seeking ways to put feet to their desire to live an obedient Christian life.

Cartoons—Why is it that everyone gets a kick out of wholesome cartoons? It's probably the combination of humor and amusing illustrations. Incorporating this visual aid into your service via the use of a projector or overhead not only captures everyone's attention, but can also be an effective way to drive home a point and make sure it sticks throughout the week. For example, if your church decided to run a series, "Ethics in the Workplace," you might consider incorporating a funny caption from the popular Dilbert comic strip. People will remember the humor and hopefully, in turn, also recall what the sermon was about.

Character—You could preach a sermon about the life of Abraham or Moses. That would be very interesting and you'd do a great job. But what if, instead, you tried a monologue, so to speak, and actually acted as if you were Abraham? Wouldn't it be captivating for your congregation to meet him and hear about his experiences firsthand? Imagine the intensity they'd feel as they related to his incredible struggle in being asked to sacrifice Isaac. Your congregation would be enthralled! Becoming the character is a great way to boost any sermon. Plus, there's that little added benefit—it really does help diminish the constant watch checking to see how much longer until the service ends!

Discussion Groups—"Let's break into small groups of six to ten and share ways you've seen God at work in your life these past few weeks." Have you ever said something like that from the pulpit? Giving people three minutes or so to discuss a relevant question is one way to get them involved in your sermon topic as well as imprinting the topic in their minds. During your sermon, consider providing an interactive opportunity for the sharing of thoughts, ideas, and experiences. After a few times of implementing this Sermon Booster, you'll find that your people will look forward to these opportunities to break out of the usual sermon format.

Dress—Have you ever preached while wearing bib overalls? No? Well, why not? If your sermon topic is "Building a Strong Foundation," you could dress in your Sunday best and preach in the clothes you normally wear. That's what everyone expects anyway. But to emphasize the importance of the topic, why not be dressed as a construction worker? As you step up to the podium, people will be wondering why you're wearing overalls and have a tool belt around your waist. Instantly you have everyone's attention as you begin preaching.

Environment—Say the sermon for this week is titled, "Reaching Out to the Lost in Our Community." Since coffee shops seem to be popular meeting places in many communities, why not arrange your sanctuary platform to resemble one? To the left of the podium you could set a circular table complete with tablecloth and a few mugs. There could even be a couple sitting at the table drinking coffee. During the sermon, whoever is speaking could walk over and sit down at another table while also giving suggestions on how to connect and develop relationships with others. Next, a waitress might walk over, pour the speaker a refill, and walk off. This is what we call creating a Sermon Booster Environment. The environment on the platform is meant to enhance and complement what's being said in the sermon. The coffee shop scene illustrates a great example of where you can go to connect with people who might not know Jesus.

Interruptions—Have you ever awakened in a cold sweat? Had that dream again, didn't you? No, not the one where you realize you're preaching naked on the platform! Come on, you know which one we're talking about. There you are preaching and someone in the congregation unexpectedly stands up and begins to question a point you've just made in your sermon. Whew! Good thing you always wake up before you have to answer, huh? Well, you don't have to sweat it anymore.

Planned interruptions that are made to look spontaneous are a great way to keep people focused on the sermon topic. Plus, you should see the looks on the people's faces when someone pops up, out of the blue, and asks a question. What a surprise—that is until they realize the inquirer was planted! That's right, the whole thing is a setup. But believe us, it works. The interruption doesn't have to be a big deal either; it can be as simple as asking one question to clarify a point.

Interview—A powerful way to capture a good story or life lesson is to interview the ones who have experienced it firsthand. During the sermon, instead of retelling the story, ask someone to share his or her experiences. The great thing about interviews is that you control them. Handing the podium over to someone is a bit risky. For one thing, you don't know how long the person is going to talk! Few people have a good instinct about time. And what do you do if they never really hit the point you wanted made? Or how were you to know the person sharing was going to "freeze" behind the podium?

But, by conducting an interview, the advantages are on your side. You, the interviewer, decide what the questions are and how many to ask. You set the tone. Plus, by asking the questions, you're putting the person interviewed at ease. Now all the interviewee has to do is simply respond to a few questions by sharing the experiences that have impacted his or her life.

Movement—Where do you stand when you deliver your sermon? What do you do with your arms? Your hands? Your feet? Have you ever had the urge to trounce across the stage to make a point? Well, why didn't you? Your instincts to do so were probably correct.

Incorporating movement into your sermons can bring a newfound life and excitement to your preaching. It's easy to get stuck behind the podium, right where you can see your sermon notes. But the simple act of moving out from behind the pulpit can emphasize your passion for the topic while also allowing you to really connect with the people to whom you're speaking. Moving around clearly says, "I really want you to hear what I'm saying."

At the same time, don't underestimate the ways you could incorporate movement into your sermon. It doesn't have to be limited to walking across the platform or standing next to instead of behind the podium. Try beginning your sermon from the back of the sanctuary or even completely out of sight of your people. Why not enter from the back and walk right down the middle aisle while preaching? (Of course, you'll likely need a cordless microphone.)

Adding movement to your sermon can deliver a punch that drives the message home. It's one way to communicate confidence and excitement. Plus, it helps capture the hearts and attention of your congregation.

Object Lesson—Wrap the thread once around your young volunteer's wrists. "Okay, try and break out of it," you challenge him. Of course, he easily does. Then you proceed to wrap it around a few more times. This time it's a little harder for him to break free. Finally, you've wrapped his wrists ten to fifteen times. He struggles. He tugs and he pulls, but he can't even budge the thin little string. "What's the matter?" you goad him on. "It's only a tiny thread. Can't you break through?" During your sermon, you use this object lesson to convey how even a small sin will eventually wrap you up and bind you.

Object lessons are most often used during the children's sermon. By why limit them? Visual and physical illustrations truly capture people's attention. After all, often it's the parents who comment on how much they appreciated the thought-provoking message for the kids. Object lessons stick. People learn from them. Christ Jesus used them all the time—a coin in a fish's mouth, baskets of leftover bread, a basin and a towel. So go ahead and give them a try. Incorporate a simple object lesson into your adult sermon. You'll be happily surprised at the positive comments you'll receive and how people will remember the point of the lesson throughout the week.

Panel Discussion—If one speaker is good, wouldn't three or four be even better? That's true when you use a panel discussion as part of your sermon. Invite three or four others (who have already been asked ahead of time) to come up to the platform. Try to choose members with varying ages, backgrounds, and experiences. Begin by moderating a brief discussion that relates to your sermon topic. This is a great way to liven up the sermon and also give your people a healthy model of what it means to disagree agreeably. By having just a few members share their thoughts, others will leave church also inspired to discuss their opinions on the topic.

Prayer—Having your entire congregation pray together sometime in the worship service is probably not uncommon. But during the sermon, have you ever had them split into groups of three to five to pray together? Sometimes this is an appropriate way to get everyone refocused on the topic. Or maybe you could predetermine a few members who would be willing to stand and pray aloud for the church. Calls to worship can incorporate prayer in revitalizing ways. In one church near a university with many internationals, different folk rose to their feet and began praying in their native tongues. The Sermon Booster emphasized that our God has a global mindset. The prayer time at the start, during, or end of a sermon can be an energizing and revitalizing tool for focusing your people on what God has to say to them through the sermon.

Sound Effects—Okay, the series this month is called, "Hiding Your Sins from God." Want to get your congregation's attention? As you physically tiptoe across the platform, acting as if you are hiding from God, have your sound person hit the play button on a cassette you've already cued. Now instead of just the visual representation of tiptoeing around, you also have the echoing sounds of footsteps walking across a loud creaking floor. If that doesn't wake up the guy in the last row, nothing will!

Storytelling—A good storyteller can capture an audience and make them hope the story will never end. That's an important gift for a pastor to master! The art of storytelling uses many different techniques—from the level of one's voice to the pacing of the tale. Storytelling is more than just communicating clearly—it's jumping into the task with total commitment.

Word on the Street (WOTS)—This minute-long video segment developed by The Chapel Ministries and Mainstay Church Resources brings the thoughts, attitudes, and opinions of the everyday people you're trying to reach right into your church. Word on the Street is a fast-moving video clip that quickly cuts from one person's viewpoint to the next, each answering the same question. Using WOTS within the context of the sermon will instantly grab your congregation's attention and force them to deal with the theme of the day. Why? Because they'll be intrigued to see what the secular culture thinks it means to pray to God, to be a Christian, or to forgive someone. Hearing viewpoints like these will undoubtedly remind your congregation of the fact that the world is utterly lost and confused. It's a great way to inspire your people to reach out to others.

Word on the Street will do just that and more. Call Mainstay Church Resources at 1-800-2-CHAPEL to find out more about how your church can order Word on the Street videos that were produced by an award-winning team of television broadcasters. But don't hesitate to send a willing person from your congregation out onto "the beat" in your town, armed with enthusiasm and a video camera. The results may surprise you!

In closing this chapter, remember you can capture the imagination and attention of your people with these simple, creative communication techniques called Sermon Boosters. As you've noticed, many are not all that different from what you're already doing. Others may require a bit more stretching when it comes to your personal comfort zone. The bottom line is to effectively communicate the message God places upon your heart. To do this, you must reach your people using techniques that speak to where they are living.

We feel that most of these Mood Setter and Sermon Booster ideas have broad application for a wide range of church styles. You may be part of a liturgical tradition or leading a "seeker sensitive" congregation, but we have found in our focus groups that most of these concepts are cross-denominationally applicable. They can be employed in varied regional settings. They cut across educational and economic distinctions. You are the one who must sensitively choose what works best for you and your people.

Our prayer is that as you choose from the Mood Setters and Sermon Boosters that follow, your worship services will be enhanced and your congregation will learn to celebrate Jesus in new and exciting ways!

CHAPTER THREE

Prayer:
The Spiritual Connection

Theme 1

Connecting Through Prayer—John 17:1–26

Related Topics: intercession, unity in the church, glorifying God, the heart of Christ

Theme 2

Connecting Through the Word—Matthew 4:1–11

Related Topics: temptation, holiness, godly character, choices, self-control, spiritual testing, Satan, power for living

Theme 3

Connecting Through Solitude—Mark 1:29–39

Related Topics: healing, priorities, power for ministry, devotions

Theme 4

Thematic Service

Jesus Stayed Spiritually Connected and Directed—John 17:1–26

Theme 1

Connecting Through Prayer

John 17:1–26

After Jesus said this, he looked toward heaven and prayed: "Father, the time has come. Glorify your Son, that your Son may glorify you. For you granted him authority over all people that he might give eternal life to all those you have given him. Now this is eternal life: that they may know you, the only true God, and Jesus Christ, whom you have sent. I have brought you glory on earth by completing the work you gave me to do. And now, Father, glorify me in your presence with the glory I had with you before the world began.

"I have revealed you to those whom you gave me out of the world. They were yours; you gave them to me and they have obeyed your word. Now they know that everything you have given me comes from you. For I gave them the words you gave me and they accepted them. They knew with certainty that I came from you, and they believed that you sent me. I pray for them. I am not praying for the world, but for those you have given me, for they are yours. All I have is yours, and all you have is mine. And glory has come to me through them. I will remain in the world no longer, but they are still in the world, and I am coming to you. Holy Father, protect them by the power of your name—the name you gave me—so that they may be one as we are one. While I was with them, I protected them and kept them safe by that name you gave me. None has been lost except the one doomed to destruction so that Scripture would be fulfilled.

"I am coming to you now, but I say these things while I am still in the world, so that they may have the full measure of my joy within them. I have given them your word and the world has hated them, for they are not of the world any more than I am of the world. My prayer is not that you take them out of the world but that you protect them from the evil one. They are not of the world, even as I am not of it. Sanctify them by the truth; your word is truth. As you sent me into the world, I have sent them into the world. For them I sanctify myself, that they too may be truly sanctified.

"My prayer is not for them alone. I pray also for those who will believe in me through their message, that all of them may be one, Father, just as you are in me and I am in you. May they also be in us so that the world may believe that you have sent me. I have given them the glory that you gave me, that they may be one as we are one: I in them and you in me. May they be brought to complete unity to let the world know that you sent me and have loved them even as you have loved me.

"Father, I want those you have given me to be with me where I am, and to see my glory, the glory you have given me because you loved me before the creation of the world.

"Righteous Father, though the world does not know you, I know you, and they know that you have sent me. I have made you known to them, and will continue to make you known in order that the love you have for me may be in them and that I myself may be in them."

Mood  Setters

Setting	Idea
Announcements	• A drama person plays the part of Lilly Tomlin's phone operator character from the '70s TV comedy, *Laugh In*. She takes phone calls in a nasal sounding voice. Each call she responds to would be one of the church announcements for that week. To help incorporate the overall service theme, have her answer each call by saying, "Thank you for calling the Prayer Line! How may I connect you?"
Building and Grounds	• Hang a banner outside the church building or in the lobby that reads, "The Prayer Line."

Mood ⓘ Setters cont.

Setting	Idea
Bulletin	• Each bulletin has a piece of a large jigsaw puzzle taped to it. Explain that, like the pieces of a jigsaw puzzle, our prayer lives are what keep us connected to the Lord. And, by also praying for each other, we are better able to stay connected in the body. When the church is connected in this way, we are playing our part in helping to complete the beautiful picture that God is putting together for our lives. Ask people to take the jigsaw piece home with them: to stick it in their pockets, wallets, or Bibles as a reminder to stay connected through prayer.
Drama	• Have two people (a man and a woman) perform *The Rehearsal* by Doug and Melissa Timberlake (available in script or on video). This witty, high-energy comedy about a director and his ditzy starlet drives home the point that it is necessary to stay connected if you want to be directed. This spiritual truth also applies to the relationship with our heavenly Father.
Greeters and Ushers	• Greeters and ushers wear headsets with microphone attachments as a visual way to set up the sermon theme of "Connecting Through Prayer." Use actual working headsets and microphones, or create makeshift ones. This could be done by using a common stereo headphone and a popsicle stick with a piece of foam attached to the end to represent the microphone piece. Buttons or T-shirts with the phrase "Get connected" would also be a nice touch for the greeters and ushers to wear.
Lighting	• Dim the lights as people enter to encourage an attitude of prayer.
Lobby	• Play a tape of "Bind Us Together" or "We Are One in the Spirit" in the lobby as people enter. (See hymnal.) • Set up a large wooden cross in the lobby. Provide 3 x 5 cards and pencils for people to write prayer requests. They may then tack them to the cross. These requests may be prayed for later in the service or passed on to a prayer team.
Music	• The choir begins a piece that sounds awful—they are off beat and out of sync because a director is not present for them to follow. At some point early in the song, have the choir director walk out and stop the chaos. He/she then begins the same song again. This time, the entire choir starts on the same beat and the same note. Use this example to later illustrate that, in

Mood 🕯 Setters cont.

Setting	Idea
Music, cont.	order to be directed, we need to stay focused on and connected with our heavenly Conductor, Jesus. One way for us to stay connected to Jesus is through prayer. The outcome will be a beautifully unified church and a minimal amount of chaos.
Offering	• As the offering is being taken, have a slide show display snapshots of marriages within your church that have lasted many years. While the slides are projected, consider also incorporating either the special music or an appropriate worship CD. Use photos of the couples' wedding pictures and also more contemporary ones showing how they look today. Sometime during the service, interview the couples about their marriage. Ask them to share how prayer helped them stay connected to God and to each other. • Use the offering time to take a collection of special prayer requests to be prayed for later in the service.
Performance Art	• Form a tableau of three groups of people in various prayer postures on the platform. The performers should take their places ten minutes before the service begins. Use the lighting to silhouette each character against the background, leaving the details of their faces obscured. Each group would illustrate one of the three parts of Jesus' prayer in the John 17:1–26 passage. For example, the person who demonstrates Jesus praying for himself could be on his knees with head bowed low and hands folded. The second group demonstrates Jesus praying for his disciples. Two people bow toward the Jesus character who has his hands placed on their heads. The third group demonstrates Jesus praying for the church. Here the Jesus character could outstretch his hands or place them on a globe.
Power Point	• List prayer needs of the church that people can pray for as they wait for the service to begin.
Prayer	• Plan a time for your congregation to pray together. Ask people to hold the hand of another as a sign of being connected while connecting with God through prayer.
Prelude	• Play a prerecorded audio tape of concerns that church members can pray for as they wait for the service to begin. Create an atmosphere that lends itself to prayer by playing soft background music.

Mood (i) Setters cont.

Setting	Idea
Sound Effects	• As the congregation enters the sanctuary, play sounds of dial tones, operators, busy signals, dialing, connecting to the Internet, etc. These sounds effects would help introduce the "connecting" theme of the day.
Visual Art	• Create a display that hangs in the lobby made up of curly telephone cords and various types of receivers. Title the display with something like, "Stay Connected." • In the church lobby, display a painting of Jesus praying on a hillside. • Display a collage of contemporary communication methods in the lobby or on the platform. For example, cell phones, beepers, a computer with e-mail, cordless phones, etc. • Take pictures of individuals and small groups in your congregation a week or two in advance (prayer groups, small groups, women or men meeting together, etc.). Make a large outline of a heart out of construction paper to be placed on the front wall of the sanctuary. Scan the pictures into Power Point and project them onto the heart, use a slide projector with a dissolve unit, or simply videotape them. Projecting these images onto the heart will illustrate that what's important to the heart of God can be seen in the prayers of his people. • As an adaptation of the above idea, take pictures of individuals and groups in your congregation a week or two in advance. Cut a large heart out of construction paper or felt and place it on the wall in the lobby. Attach the pictures onto the heart to illustrate the same idea.

Sermon (💡) Boosters

Booster	Idea
Action Step	• Invite the congregation to stand and hold hands after the message. Lead them in a chorus of "Bind Us Together." (See hymnal.)
Character	• The pastor dresses like writer George Mueller. He could talk from his point of view about the importance of staying connected to God through the power of prayer. Use his biography to pull stories from his life that would illustrate the key sermon points.

Sermon 💡 Boosters cont.

Booster	Idea
Environment	• Set the platform to resemble the Last Supper because Jesus' prayer in John 17:1–26 took place during the last week of his life. A simple wooden table with a broken loaf of bread and a pottery cup would set the scene. The pastor could preach in this environment to illustrate his/her sermon points.
Interruption	• If you've been using the telephone as a thematic motif to illustrate staying connected, carry it on into the sermon time. As the pastor is preaching, have his/her cell phone ring. He/she finds the phone, and then explains to the congregation that this is a call that is going to have to be taken. When the pastor answers the call, the congregation realizes that God is the caller and he wants the pastor to clarify a few of the sermon points. Someone with a deep voice could play the voice of God off-stage.
Object Lesson	• Toss an extra large ball of yarn into the congregation. The pastor should hold one end of the yarn and ask the congregation to throw the ball from one part of the sanctuary to those sitting in another section. As the ball unravels people should take hold of a section of the yarn. This should continue until all the yarn is unwound. Explain that just as this ball of yarn has connected people together, prayer does the same thing—only better! Emphasize the importance of every part of the congregation being connected one to another through prayer.
	• Using two tin cans and a string, demonstrate how to build a simple kids' telephone. Use this object lesson to make the point that beginning a prayer life is as simple as modeling a child who is talking on a mock telephone. It doesn't take a lot of effort, just a willingness to make a simple connection to God.
	• Lead a row of the congregation in playing the "telephone game." One person says a simple sentence to another and then this sentence is whispered from one person to the next. When the sentence has finally reached the last person, he/she speaks aloud what was heard. Then, have the first person say aloud what the original sentence was. Almost always the sentence has changed as it has been repeated from one person to the next. The pastor would then explain how vitally important it is to stay in touch with God through prayer. If we lose our connection with him, our messages and thinking very quickly become confused and off track. Staying in touch with Jesus keeps us from experiencing the "telephone effect" in our

Sermon ☉ Boosters cont.

Booster	Idea
Object Lesson, cont.	spiritual lives. Prayer is a direct line to God. Our prayers are clearly understood. God doesn't ever get the sentences all mixed up as was illustrated by the "telephone game." • While the pastor preaches, he/she begins cutting out paper dolls to illustrate how we're all connected in the body of Christ. Insert a variety of colored paper to represent various races. Or, use printed paper to illustrate that there are many different kinds of people in the body of Christ. Unfold the paper dolls to visually emphasize the importance of staying connected through prayer. • The pastor shows the congregation a painted wooden nesting doll. As he/she takes off the top half, another smaller doll is revealed inside. He does this several times, each time revealing another smaller doll inside. Use this to illustrate Jesus' point, "that they may be one as we are one." • The pastor refers to a computer system that is already set up on the platform. He/she talks about how amazing computers are in connecting us to the world. The pastor then also talks about how amazing prayer is in keeping us connected to God.
Panel Discussion	• Gather a group of people to discuss how prayer has helped them stay connected to God and connected to church. They might also want to be a bit vulnerable and talk about the times when they weren't connected to God through prayer and what those times felt like.
Prayer	• Divide the sermon into three parts based upon the three parts of Jesus' prayer. Follow each part of the sermon with a time of prayer and a chorus. For example: Prayer for ourselves, Prayer for followers of Christ, Prayer for those who will become Christians. • As the pastor finishes a point in the sermon, he/she asks the congregation to gather in groups of three or four for prayer. Ask the groups to lift up prayers that would reflect their desire to be more connected as the body of Christ.
WOTS	• Go into your community and ask the question, "How often do you pray and what does prayer mean to you?" • Videotape people's responses to the question, "What does unity mean to you?" • Videotape people's responses to the question, "How do you stay spiritually connected to God?"

Theme 2

Connecting Through the Word

Matthew 4:1–11

Then Jesus was led by the Spirit into the desert to be tempted by the devil. After fasting forty days and forty nights, he was hungry. The tempter came to him and said, "If you are the Son of God, tell these stones to become bread."

Jesus answered, "It is written: 'Man does not live on bread alone, but on every word that comes from the mouth of God.'"

Then the devil took him to the holy city and had him stand on the highest point of the temple. "If you are the Son of God," he said, "throw yourself down. For it is written: 'He will command his angels concerning you, and they will lift you up in their hands, so that you will not strike your foot against a stone.'"

Jesus answered him, "It is also written: 'Do not put the Lord your God to the test.'"

Again, the devil took him to a very high mountain and showed him all the kingdoms of the world and their splendor. "All this I will give you," he said, "if you will bow down and worship me."

Jesus said to him, "Away from me, Satan! For it is written: 'Worship the Lord your God, and serve him only.'"

Then the devil left him, and angels came and attended him.

Mood  Setters

Setting	Idea
Announcements	• The person doing the announcements has two people standing on either side of him or her. One person is dressed like a devil and the other is dressed like an angel. The devil tempts the announcer, whispering things like, "Don't go to the Monday night Bible study! Stay home and watch Monday night football instead." The angel responds, "Don't listen to him! Go to the Monday night Bible study. Take time to delve into the Word and feed your spirit." The announcer ends up being pulled in two different directions. We may not really know what he/she will choose to do.
Aroma	• Permeate the sanctuary with the smell of baking bread to help people understand the powerful allure food can have. Refer to this mood setter during the sermon to help people understand the way Satan was tempting Jesus.
Building and Grounds	• Using bricks, outline a "fork in the road" on the walkway into the church. Refer to this later in the service as an object lesson of the choices we have to make when we are tempted. • Indicate a "fork in the road" on the walkway into the church using footsteps cut out of construction paper or plastic. Have the footstep pattern split into two different directions. Later in the service, challenge the congregation to choose to walk in the footsteps of Jesus when they are tempted.

Mood 🕯 Setters cont.

Setting	Idea
Building and Grounds, cont.	• Someone dresses as a carnival barker and stands outside of the entrance to the church, enticing people to, "Step right up! Step this way! Get the latest temptation! I've got all the latest and greatest for you right here! Step over this way!" • Make three banners to hang outside the entrance to the building. Print one of Jesus' responses to the devil on each one. (See Matthew 4:4, 7, 10.)
Bulletin	• Design the bulletin to look like a circus flyer. "Today's MAIN EVENT: Every Temptation Under the Big Top."
Handout	• At the end of the service, distribute an item with the popular "WWJD?" (What Would Jesus Do?) on it. For example, give a bookmark or bracelet. Suggest that people use it as a reminder to do as Jesus did by using Scripture to refute temptation.
Introduction	• Introduce the concept of Jesus being tested by giving the congregation a "test." Ask simple questions such as, "What's one area of temptation in your life?" or "How do you typically respond when faced with temptation?" Suggest that people choose to combat their temptations by memorizing and quoting Scripture as Jesus did. • Fill the sanctuary with the smell of freshly baked bread. The person doing the introduction enters the platform eating a piece of the bread, describing how wonderful it tastes. "Oh, this bread baked by Shelley [name a well-known good cook in your church] is so-o good! Mmm, I just wish I could share it with you." A person planted in the congregation says, "I can't take it any more! That bread smells so good. It looks like it would taste just great—and I'm so hungry! Give me a piece of your bread!" The person doing the introduction says, "Oh, I don't have a piece of bread for you, but I do have these stones. If you really had faith, you could command them to turn into bread." "Hey, you almost got me there," the person in the congregation says. "But I know better. Jesus says, 'Man does not live on bread alone, but on every word that comes from the mouth of God.'"
Lobby	• Set out a display of items that would be tempting to people as they enter, such as bowls of candy. Place signs next to them that read: "Do Not Touch!" • Set up orange parking cones throughout the lobby. On the top of each one, attach a sign with a temptation printed on it. For

Mood 🕯 Setters cont.

Setting	Idea
Lobby, cont.	example, "Lust," "Pride," "Greed," "Power." Set them up in such a way that people have to walk around them to get to their destination.
Reading	• Select an excerpt from the classic book by C.S.Lewis, *Screwtape Letters,* where the demons talk about how to tempt their subjects. The excerpt chosen may be read by one or more persons.
Video	• Show a clip from a video by Carmen called, *Satan, Bite the Dust.*
Visual Art	• Design an image of a fork in the road to be displayed on the back wall of the platform or on a board in the lobby. • Display a montage of oversized objects that signify various kinds of temptations. For example: money, pictures of houses and cars, a large business card with "C.E.O." printed on it. Juxtapose these with quotes from Jesus to the devil (see Matthew 4:4, 7, 10). The pastor or someone else may point out that while there is nothing wrong with these things in and of themselves, they can become temptations for us if we worship them more than God.

Sermon 💡 Boosters

Booster	Idea
Action Step	• Using the popular slogan/question, "What Would Jesus Do?" (WWJD?) ask people to consider how they can do what Jesus did when facing temptation. Emphasize refuting temptation with Scripture by handing out Scripture memory cards with Jesus' responses to the devil printed on them. Print "What Would Jesus Do?" across the top of the cards. You could also have blank cards that people could use to write verses of Scripture that would specifically apply to their areas of struggle with temptation. • Insert a sheet into the bulletin that lists areas of temptation. Ask the congregation to prayerfully mark those areas that are a struggle for them. Print Jesus' three responses across the bottom of the page (see Matthew 4:4, 7, 10). Also include

Sermon Boosters cont.

Booster	Idea
Action Step, cont.	other verses that may be used to combat a "Signature Sin," such as 1 Corinthians 10:13. • Challenge the congregation to memorize Jesus' responses to the devil (Matthew 4:4, 7, 10).
Cartoon	• Show a cartoon of a person with a devil on one shoulder and an angel on the other, both trying to get him to follow their advice. You may show the cartoon on an overhead transparency, slide, or Power Point.
Environment	• Fill the sanctuary with the smell of freshly baked bread. The aroma will make the congregation begin to feel hungry. The pastor can refer to this when preaching on the portion of the passage where Jesus is tempted to turn the stones into bread. Remind the congregation that Jesus hadn't eaten for forty days and was very hungry. • Create a two-sided environment on the platform. One side is filled with objects that represent areas of temptation and the other side is filled with objects that represent things that lead to life. The pastor should move between the two environments as he/she preaches.
Interruption	• Play a voice-over of the devil tempting the pastor as he/she preaches: "Why don't you just sit down. You have nothing to say to these people. Besides, you're so full of pride. And what about yesterday, when you hollered at your kids? What kind of a pastor are you? Hey, why don't you just cut it short this morning? Your congregation would love you if you did. Then you could go play golf!" • Two people dressed as a devil and an angel interrupt the pastor. They stand on opposite sides of him/her, pulling in two different directions as they attempt to get the pastor to follow them.
Sound Effects	• Insert sound effects while the pastor reads the Scripture. For example, while the devil speaks, play dissonant music or a sound like fingers scraping on a blackboard. While Jesus responds, change to soothing, calming music.
Storytelling	• Tell the story of an incident that occurred in Poland during World War II. People were given bread made out of sawdust. It looked, tasted, and smelled like bread, but had no nutritional

Sermon ⚙ Boosters cont.

Booster	Idea
Storytelling, cont.	value. As a result, people died from lack of nutrition although they had full stomachs. The same truth applies to us today. We can fill ourselves with things that look tempting but have no lasting, life-giving value.
Video	• Show a clip from the film, *Wall Street*, where Michael Douglas delivers a monologue on greed. Use the insert to illustrate what evil looks like when we give in to temptations like greed, etc. • When the pastor talks about how sin and temptation may not always appear as the evil they really are, show a video of images morphing from one to another.
WOTS	• Go into the community and videotape responses to the questions, "What's your greatest temptation?" or "How do you handle temptation?" • Videotape kids' responses to the question, "What gets you in trouble?"

Theme 3

Connecting Through Solitude

Mark 1:29–39

As soon as they left the synagogue, they went with James and John to the home of Simon and Andrew. Simon's mother-in-law was in bed with a fever, and they told Jesus about her. So he went to her, took her hand and helped her up. The fever left her and she began to wait on them.

That evening after sunset the people brought to Jesus all the sick and demon-possessed. The whole town gathered at the door, and Jesus healed many who had various diseases. He also drove out many demons, but he would not let the demons speak because they knew who he was.

Very early in the morning, while it was still dark, Jesus got up, left the house and went off to a solitary place, where he prayed. Simon and his companions went to look for him, and when they found him, they exclaimed: "Everyone is looking for you!"

Jesus replied, "Let us go somewhere else—to the nearby villages—so I can preach there also. That is why I have come."
So he traveled throughout Galilee, preaching in their synagogues and driving out demons.

Mood 🕯 Setters

Setting	Idea
Building and Grounds	• Park two cars near the entrance to the church. Connect them with jumper cables. Place a sign near the cars that reads, "Get Connected."
Greeters and Ushers	• Greeters and ushers wear buttons that read "Get Connected, Stay Directed." Print the words over a watermark impression of praying hands.
Lighting/ Performance Art	• Dim the lights in the sanctuary for the beginning of the service. Focus a spotlight on a solitary person in a posture of prayer on the platform. Focus another light from the person praying up to a cross on the back wall of the platform.
Lobby	• Display a sign at the entrance to the sanctuary that reads, "Quiet please as you enter the sanctuary. This morning, take this opportunity for prayer and meditation."
Prelude	• Play an audio tape of various people praying as an opening to the service. These should be short, one-sentence prayers by people of all different ages and genders. If possible, incorporate people with different nationalities as well. It would be effective to have the voices fade in and out and overlap when appropriate.

Mood  Setters cont.

Setting	Idea
Prelude/Transition Music	• Play "Seek Ye First" as the prelude (Karen Lafferty, in *The Hymnal for Worship and Celebration*). Weave it throughout the service for the various transitions between service elements. End the service with the congregational chorus of the more upbeat, "Seek First," from *Songs from the Loft*, Reunion Records.
Sound Effects	• In the lobby, play an audio tape of nature sounds to set the mood of an early morning. Later in the service, bring the sound effect back into the sermon time as the pastor points out that Jesus arose early, while it was still dark, to pray.
Video	• Show the video, *On My Knees*, by Jaci Valasquez, published by Myrrh.
Visual Arts	• Display a montage of various sources of power either in the lobby or on the back wall of the platform. Include such things as batteries, solar panels, jumper cables, electrical cords, etc.

Sermon ⚙ Boosters

Booster	Idea
Discussion Groups	• Divide the congregation into groups of five or six and discuss the question, "How do you stay spiritually connected?" If you use a Word on the Street segment which answers this same question, the discussion groups could follow just after the video is shown.
Environment	• Create the environment of a living room, study, or place where people might go to have a quiet time. Use this to help people understand that finding a special place to talk to God where they won't be interrupted is an important part of staying connected.
Interruption	• Plant people in the congregation with pagers and cell phones that they can make ring at a predetermined time. The pastor can use these planned interruptions as an object lesson concerning how busy and intrusive our technological world has become. He/she should point out that in order to talk to God, we must free ourselves from the distractions around us.

Sermon Boosters cont.

Booster	Idea
Interruption, cont.	• The sound person runs down the aisle to fix the pastor's microphone. This person should be apologizing for interrupting, but explaining that with today's technology, things still go wrong and interruptions often do happen. • The pastor receives an important cell phone call in the middle of the sermon. The call can be from God. Use this conversation to communicate some of the things God desires during our quiet times.
Interview	• Interview someone from the church who has a strong prayer life and can express and share times when he/she has been directed through prayer.
Movement	• While preaching, the pastor wanders off the platform into a side room or closet. By doing this, he/she demonstrates that the important thing about talking to God is being able to separate yourself from the distractions that pull your thoughts and attention. Of course, the pastor should have a cordless microphone so the people can still hear him/her talking.
Panel Discussion	• Have a panel discussion made up of drama people who would play the roles of a few of the disciples. Ask them to explain why they thought Jesus left early in the morning to go and pray to God. Also discuss why finding a place of solitude was so important to Jesus.
WOTS	• Videotape people's responses to the questions, "How do you stay spiritually connected?" and "Do you pray?"

Thematic Service

Theme 4

Jesus Stayed Spiritually Connected and Directed

John 17:1–26

Mood ⓘ Setter

Form a tableau of three groups of people in various prayer postures on the platform. The performers should take their places ten minutes before the service begins. The lighting should be such that the characters are silhouetted against the background with the details of their faces obscured. Each group would illustrate one of the three parts of Jesus' prayer. For example, the person who demonstrates Jesus praying for himself could be on his knees with head bowed low and hands folded. The second group demonstrates Jesus praying for his disciples. Two people bow toward the Jesus character who has his hands placed on their heads. The third group demonstrates Jesus praying for the church. Here the Jesus character could outstretch his hands or place them on a globe.

PRELUDE

Play an audio tape of concerns for people to pray for as they wait for the service to begin. Add to the atmosphere of prayer by playing soft background music.

WELCOME, PRAISE, AND WORSHIP 13 minutes

ANNOUNCEMENTS 4 minutes

DRAMA 5 minutes

"The Rehearsal" (Doug and Melissa Timberlake, Mainstay Church Resources)

OFFERING 3 minutes

MESSAGE WITH WOTS 30 minutes

"Is it hard to pray consistently?" ("Word on the Street," *Mood Setters and Sermon Boosters*, Mainstay Church Resources)*

SPECIAL MUSIC 5 minutes

"Listen to Our Hearts" (Geoff Moore and the Distance)

CHORUS 3 minutes

"Show Me Your Ways"

CHORUS 3 minutes

"Turn Your Eyes upon Jesus"

(Total Service Time **66 minutes**)

---

* To obtain these resources, see the resource section on page 186.

REMEMBER

- Adapt these services to fit your worship style. Choose the elements that will communicate best to your congregation.
- Don't mix metaphors when selecting service elements.
- Change the times for each element to suit your needs.
- Substitute music or dramatic elements to suit your setting.
- Think through the flow from element to element. Transitions can be as simple as a phrase or two by a worship leader or other service participant.

Additional Resources

Overall Topic: Prayer: The Spiritual Connection

Suggested Dramas

Drama Title	Author	Publisher
"The Rehearsal"	The Timberlakes	Mainstay Church Resources
"Dear Babby"	The Timberlakes	Mainstay Church Resources
"Hard Choices: Three Prayers"	The Timberlakes John Yarbrough	Mainstay Church Resources
"Heroes of Faith"	Robert Lackie	Mainstay Church Resources
"Honest to God"	Deborah Craig Claar	Word Publishers
"No Interruptions"	Sharon Sherbondy	Zondervan ChurchSource
"Quiet Time"	Sharon Sherbondy	Zondervan ChurchSource
"It's a Lie"	Kelly Wick	Creative Resource Group

Suggested Special Music

Song	Artist	Compact Disc	Label
"Listen to Our Hearts"	Geoff Moore and the Distance	*Evolution*	Forefront Communications
"Midnight Oil"	Phillips, Craig & Dean	*Phillips, Craig and Dean*	StarSong
"Shelter"	Jaci Valesquez	*Heavenly Place*	Myrrh
"In the Wilderness"	Michael James	*Shoulder to the Wind*	Reunion
"Deep Is Our Hunger"	Michael James	*Shoulder to the Wind*	Reunion
"Enter In"	Chuck Girard	*Fire & Light*	Word

Suggested Special Music, cont.

Song	Artist	Compact Disc	Label
"Let Us Pray"	Stephen Curtis Chapman	*Signs of Life*	Sparrow
"On My Knees"	Willow Creek	*A Place to Call Home*	Word
"Verticality"	Eric Champion	*Touch*	Brentwood
"Journey"	Eric Champion	*Touch*	Brentwood
"Help Me Now"	Kathy Troccoli	*Love & Mercy*	Reunion
"Maybe Tomorrow"	Sixpence None the Richer	*This Beautiful Mess*	REX

Suggested Worship Songs

Song	Label
"Turn Your Eyes Upon Jesus"	Word
"I Just Want to Be Where You Are"	Integrity
"It Is the Cry of My Heart"	Integrity
"Nothing Is So Wonderful"	Vineyard
"Show Me Your Ways"	Hillsong/Australia
"Thy Word"	Meadowgreen

CHAPTER FOUR

Stereotypes: Shattering the Prejudice That Wounds Us

Theme 5

Stereotypes of Religious People—Luke 18:9–14

Related Topics: *pride, humility, parables, Pharisee and the tax collector, justification*

Theme 6

Stereotypes of Faith—Luke 7:1–10

Related Topics: *healing, power of Christ, trust, dependency on Christ*

Theme 7

Stereotypes of Segregation—John 4:1–42

Related Topics: *prejudice, gender discrimination, ethnic diversity, women, acceptance in Christ, evangelism, the woman at the well, identity of God*

Theme 8

Thematic Service

Jesus Shattered the Stereotypes of "Us" and "Them"—Luke 18:9–24

Related Topics: *pride, humility, parables, Pharisee and the tax collector, justification*

Theme 5

Stereotypes of Religious People

Luke 18:9–14

To some who were confident of their own righteousness and looked down on everybody else, Jesus told this parable: "Two men went up to the temple to pray, one a Pharisee and the other a tax collector. The Pharisee stood up and prayed about himself: 'God, I thank you that I am not like other men—robbers, evildoers, adulterers—or even like this tax collector. I fast twice a week and give a tenth of all I get.'

"But the tax collector stood at a distance. He would not even look up to heaven, but beat his breast and said, 'God, have mercy on me, a sinner.'

"I tell you that this man, rather than the other, went home justified before God. For everyone who exalts himself will be humbled, and he who humbles himself will be exalted."

Mood Setters

Setting	Idea
Announcements	• Two people give the announcements in a "one-up-manship" style. Each one tries to outdo the other, borrowing from the Pharisee's attitude and dialogue. For example, after the first one gives an announcement, the second person says to the congregation, "Well, I'm glad I'm not like *that* person. I'm having my car washed by the youth next Saturday morning at 10:00. And *I'm* going to attend Bible study at 7:00 every Monday night this month."
Building and Grounds	• As people approach the church, they notice a group of diverse people hanging out in front of the building. These people consist of the following groups; punkers, truckers, businessman, clergy, sports jocks, etc. Use this object lesson to help people focus on the fact that there are many different kinds of people and customs. One is no better than the other. What is in people's hearts is most important. Explain that the same was true of the Pharisee and the tax collector. • Make a banner to hang outside the entrance of the building which reads, "Humble Thyself in the Sight of the Lord."
Cartoon	• Show a cartoon from the "Peanuts" comic strip. Choose one with Lucy being particularly puffed up and Charlie Brown being humble.
Communion	• Use scruffy-looking ushers to offset the look of the Pharisee usher described below in the Ushers and Greeters section. When it comes time for communion, have these scruffy ushers

Mood (i) Setters cont.

Setting	Idea
Communion, cont.	come forward and take off their mangy coats and shirts to reveal a white outfit that signifies purity. Another way to accomplish this would be to have them take off their scruffy coats and put on white robes instead.
	• Invite people to come forward and kneel to receive communion. This will be particularly effective if kneeling is not the way your church traditionally receives communion.
	• Pass the communion elements on small trays throughout the congregation. Using one loaf, each person serves the person next to him or her. The wine or juice may be served in one cup or in small cups. As the elements are passed, the server says, "The body of Christ given for you," and "The blood of Christ given for you."
Greeters and Ushers	• Greeters and ushers wear buttons that say, "Humble Yourself in the Sight of the Lord."
	• Dress one of the greeters like a Pharisee. This person would be the first to greet people, but would snub them by saying something downgrading like, "Well, they'll let anyone in a church these days!" The Pharisee should be very boisterous and animated. Have your regular ushers and greeters greet everyone after the Pharisee has played his part. During the welcome and greeting time, explain that this Pharisee is much like the one in today's Scripture passage.
Handout	• Stamp the back of people's hands as they leave the sanctuary with an "H" to help them remember the marks of humility that the tax collector showed.
	• Hand out "to-its" to people as they leave the service. These are round circles the size of a large coin. They could be made of construction paper. The word "to-it" is printed on one side. The idea is that we often say we'll serve someone else when we get "around to it." Well, here's a "round to-it" so folks have no more excuses!
Introduction	• Use animation or cartoon slides of "Pride" being smashed and "Humility" sprouting out of that.
	• The person doing the introduction tells an anecdote about a time that he encountered humility in another person. Close the introduction by reading Luke 18:9–14 from Eugene Peterson's, *The Message*.

Mood (i) Setters cont.

Setting	Idea
Introduction, cont.	• The person doing the introduction to the service reads several children's prayers as examples of humility.
Lobby	• Sew a short curtain (about four feet long by the width of your doorway). It should be long enough so that people have to bow under it to enter the sanctuary. Hang it on a rod over the entrance to the sanctuary. Print the words, "Humble Yourself" on the curtain or on a large sign.
Prelude/Postlude	• Record a tape of children praying simple, honest prayers. Play the tape as part of the prelude or at the beginning of the service. • The prelude music for today could be "Pomp and Circumstance" to reflect the attitude of the Pharisee in the story. The postlude music could be something like the chorus "Humble Thyself" to reflect the attitude of the tax collector.
Tableau	• As a narrator reads the Scripture verses, actors pantomime the scene using simple movements. These characters shouldn't interact with one another, but the Pharisee can motion toward the tax collector to show his disgust. • Place two people on the platform in a foot washing scene. They should be frozen in position. If possible, light them from the back so they appear in silhouette. Play music that fits the mood of the scene. The congregation views this scene as they enter the sanctuary. The pastor may refer to this scene later in the service as an example of humility.
Video	• Show a clip from the film, *Godspell,* of Jesus telling this parable of the Pharisee and the tax collector.
Visual Art	• Either on the back podium wall or in the lobby, your Visual Arts team (or an artist in your church) can make a silhouette outline or large poster of the Blind Justice character.
Welcome	• The person welcoming the congregation humbly steps down and invites a child to give the welcome instead. This is particularly effective if the same person usually gives the welcome each week.
Action Step	• Challenge the congregation to do a "Secret Act of Service" this week. For example, bring a sack of groceries to someone in

Sermon Boosters

Booster	Idea
Action Step, cont.	need. They should be encouraged to do these acts anonymously, as a way of being humble servants.
Character	• The pastor preaches from God's point of view as he hears the people praying the two types of prayers in Luke 18:9–14.
Discussion Groups	• Divide your congregation into groups of five to seven to discuss what it means to be humble.
Dress	• The pastor could dress in Pharisee garb during the sermon. This will help capture the attention of the congregation and imprint the message.
Interruption	• As the pastor begins the sermon, the Pharisee previously mentioned from the Ushers and Greeters section (or just someone dressed as a Pharisee) comes forward to the front row making a loud entrance and saying something like, "I should be seated in the front row! I deserve a place of high honor and respect. Nothing less is suitable. You don't expect me to sit with tax collectors and other unmentionable people do you? They all sit in the back of the sanctuary. I'm far above that!" At this point the pastor signals the rest of the ushers. They walk to the front and show the Pharisee to his seat in the back of the sanctuary.
	• Someone interrupts the pastor, bragging about how they could tell the story better.
Interview	• You could title this interview, "Confessions of a Former Pharisee." Interview someone from your congregation who has struggled with being a modern-day Pharisee, but who, through the power of God, has been set free from critically judging others.
	• Interview actors who play the parts of the Pharisee and the tax collector.
	• Interview a person who used to think of the church stereotypically, but has since changed his/her mind.
	• Interview several school-aged children in a "Kids Say the Darndest Things" style. Ask the question, "What does a Christian look like to you?"

Sermon ⚙ Boosters cont.

Booster	Idea
Movement	• When preaching the sermon, the pastor could use simple movements to help model the different positions a person can use when praying to convey an attitude of humility before the Lord (kneeling, lying prostrate, hand raised in praise, etc.).
Panel Discussion	• Gather parents of teenagers for a panel. Have them discuss the positive things about their kids, while also confronting the negative stereotypes with which teenagers are often labeled. This discussion should help break down the attitude of some that teenagers have nothing to contribute to those older than them. Explain that a spirit of humility is needed to accept the fact that we can learn from those who are younger. Jesus desires to break down the walls that separate "us" from "them." • Moderate a panel of people discussing ways they used to think they could please God and how that has or has not changed. For example, even though Christians know a person isn't saved by what they do, often we try to please God through what we do rather than simply seeking him with a humble heart.
Prayer	• The pastor talks about how prayer is an indication of the heart of a person. He/she then leads the congregation through a time of guided prayer. Encourage people to take this time to get their hearts right with God. • Lead the congregation in a time of prayer focusing on their actions. Help them become aware of their spirit of humility or lack thereof. • Two people stand in the congregation to pray aloud. The first one is obviously concerned with impressing the congregation. He/she uses very flowery church-sounding language with many thee's and thou's. The second person uses simple heartfelt language and humbles himself/herself before the Lord.

Stereotypes of Faith

Luke 7:1–10

When Jesus had finished saying all this in the hearing of the people, he entered Capernaum. There a centurion's servant, whom his master valued highly, was sick and about to die. The centurion heard of Jesus and sent some elders of the Jews to him, asking him to come and heal his servant. When they came to Jesus, they pleaded earnestly with him, "This man deserves to have you do this, because he loves our nation and has built our synagogue." So Jesus went with them.

He was not far from the house when the centurion sent friends to say to him: "Lord, don't trouble yourself, for I do not deserve to have you come under my roof. That is why I did not even consider myself worthy to come to you. But say the word, and my servant will be healed. For I myself am a man under authority, with soldiers under me. I tell this one, 'Go,' and he goes; and that one, 'Come,' and he comes. I say to my servant, 'Do this,' and he does it."

When Jesus heard this, he was amazed at him, and turning to the crowd following him, he said, "I tell you, I have not found such great faith even in Israel." Then the men who had been sent returned to the house and found the servant well.

Mood Setters

Setting	Idea
Announcements	• Dress someone as a first-century Roman centurion to give the announcements. Provide him with a scroll to read from and encourage him to speak with authority and to command the congregation to listen. • Use the person (from the Introduction listed below) who is dressed as an old-time elevator operator to give the first announcement. Continue with people coming to get on the elevator. As they do, the elevator operator asks, "Floor please?" They may respond something like "Third floor, Men's Prayer Breakfast." That person can continue on in conversation with the elevator operator, giving more details about the event. Then another person enters, requests a different floor with a corresponding event or announcement, and so on.
Building and Grounds	• Design the doors through which the congregation leaves the sanctuary to look like elevator doors. Before the service is over, make reference to the exits. Invite people to reach for the "next floor" of their ride of faith.
Drama	• Write a modern-day version of Luke 7:1–10. Use a CEO of a big corporation or a local politician to portray the role of the Roman officer.
Greeters and Ushers	• Dress your greeters and ushers as Roman centurions.

Mood  Setters cont.

Setting	Idea
Healing Ministry	• Set aside a significant portion of the service to minister to those in need of healing. This could be done any number of ways—from offering a prayer of healing over the whole congregation to inviting people to the front platform where the elders can pray over them and anoint them with oil. Be sure to allow enough time for this to take place in the service. You may be surprised how many people acknowledge their need for the Lord's healing touch.
Introduction	• Stage a faith fall where one person falls backward into the arms of a group of people. The person falling has to put his/her faith in the fact that the others *will* catch him/her. The person who made the fall would then introduce the service or series as one about putting your faith in Jesus—inviting the congregation to fall upon him for all their needs.
	• Invite a CEO from a corporation to explain the corporate structure. He/she should also tell about a time that a simple phone call got results in another city or state. The CEO should draw parallels from his/her life to the life of the centurion in Luke 7:1–10. Point out that when you are in charge, you command people and they must listen. Have the CEO explain that the centurion also knew and understood the awesome power Jesus had over his servant's illness.
	• Stage a dialogue between two people in a "Dumb and Dumber" style. One person needs to make a copy of a document. The other person suggests going to all the wrong places to have the copy made, such as a candy store or the park. He/she *really believes* that the copy can be made there. A third person then enters and sends the first two to the right place. He/she explains that it's not the amount of faith we have, but rather, the object of our faith that is the key. The object of the centurion's faith was Jesus, and that's what healed his servant.
	• Dress someone as an old-time elevator operator. He can tell a story about people from a third-world country who were told that if they stepped into an elevator and pushed 12, they would ride skyward. The "elevator operator" explains that it doesn't matter if the people *feel* confident or secure about trying what they've been told, what matters is that they act in faith, step in, and push the button. The elevator will go to the twelfth floor because that's what it was built to do, not because someone believes it will.

Mood  Setters cont.

Setting	Idea
Lobby	• While the service is in progress, place large footsteps in the lobby with the words "Steps of Faith" written on them. As people leave, invite them to follow the steps of faith out into their everyday lives.
Prelude/Postlude	• Create a voice-over of various people sharing times when they had to trust Jesus with certain circumstances in their lives. As the congregation leaves the service, the postlude could consist of these same stories but now we hear the outcome of what God did in their lives because of their faith.
Sound Effects/Transition	• Create a sound effects tape of a bell ringing, the swooshing sound of an elevator door opening and a voice saying, "Going up." Play this tape between each element of the service. Follow the sound effects tape with taped "elevator music." (Use this transition only if using other elevator motifs suggested in this section.)
Video	• Use the scene from the movie, *Contact,* where the characters discuss the idea of faith. • Play the scene from the movie, *Indiana Jones and the Temple of Doom,* where Indy has to take the step of faith in order to cross the chasm.
Visual Art	• Hang a banner that uses the word "faith" as an acronym. Your acronym might read something like: Fear not Accept Invite Trust Hope

Sermon Boosters

Booster	Idea
Action Step	• The congregation writes down their answers to the question, "In your own healing process, what areas of doubt do you struggle with?" • Give the congregation "Rules for Riding the Elevator of Faith." These would include things like, "*Do* talk to others on the elevator, don't keep your faith to yourself." "*Do* trust in the engineer who designed the elevator; don't look for a repairman before a problem arises." "Remember, even if the ride gets

Sermon 💡 Boosters cont.

Booster	Idea
Action Step, cont.	bumpy, it's still easier than climbing 28 flights of stairs." (Use your imagination to design this action step to meet the needs of your congregation.) • Place a large cross on the platform. Invite people to come up and nail their doubts to the cross as an act of putting their doubt to death. Follow this with a time of prayer, asking the Lord to bring new life to their faith.
Application	• Insert a "test" in the bulletin. Ask people to consider where they may have encountered Jesus during the past week. Consider such areas as work, family, driving, shopping, playing golf, or any place they saw faith in action or exercised faith on behalf of themselves or another. Encourage the congregation to make a conscious effort to observe these things during the next week. Then, they should compare the two weeks and notice if there are differences when making a conscious decision to encounter Jesus in faith.
Cartoon	• Charlie Brown trying to kick the football is a great illustration of a person with faith.
Discussion Groups	• Break into groups of three to five. Ask people to share times they were surprised by faith, either their own faith, or the faith of another person.
Interruption	• Ask a few people ahead of time to interrupt the pastor with specific questions about faith. (Be sure to let them know exactly when they should interrupt the sermon to pose the question.) Use these questions to introduce each new sermon point that is to be made.
Interview	• Interview an actor playing the part of the servant who was sent to deliver the Roman soldier's message to Jesus. Ask him such questions as, "Did Jesus seemed surprised?" or "What happened when you got back to the centurion's house?" • Interview a missionary about people he/she has encountered who may have seemed unlikely to be people of faith (such as, did not grow up in a Christian environment, were not well versed in the Scriptures), yet they demonstrated great faith. Ask for specific examples and stories. • Interview someone playing the part of a person in the crowd the day the centurion came to Jesus. Ask him/her to tell about

Sermon 💡 Boosters cont.

Booster	Idea
Interview, cont.	the faith of the centurion, and Jesus' response to this type of faith coming from a person outside the nation of Israel. • Interview someone who, like the centurion in the passage, has acted in faith on behalf of another person. This might be someone who prayed consistently for another who was ill, or a person who regularly gives to the needy of the community, etc.
Object Lesson	• Use a blindfold and a volunteer to illustrate the point that the person wearing the blindfold must trust the other person to not allow him/her to get hurt or into trouble. You might have a group of people standing by with a portable platform that would extend the area of the platform by an additional five or six feet. Once the person is blindfolded, the helpers silently move the additional platform into position. Once it's set, ask the blindfolded person to walk toward the end of the main platform. When this person gets to the point where he/she is sure the stage ends he/she will pause, being cautious not to step off and fall. Now the pastor will simply ask the person to take a step of faith and trust the pastor with his/her safety.
Panel Discussion	• Gather a panel of three to five people to discuss the question, "What issues of faith do you struggle with?"
Power Point	• Take an e-mail survey a few weeks in advance to find the most common answers to the question, "Who do you go to when you have a problem you can't handle?" Project the answers to the survey using Power Point. Show that most answers indicate a parent, trusted friend, counselor, or doctor. Explain that the centurion in the passage didn't waste any time. He went straight to the top and asked Jesus to heal his servant.
Storytelling	• Tell a story about being stuck in an elevator. Describe the feelings of fear, doubt, anxiety, impatience, or anger that some of the passengers felt. Describe the denial or casual attitude others expressed. Explain that in the "Elevator of Faith," the ride is not always smooth. There may even be times when the elevator comes to a screeching halt. But ultimately, the outcome is not in our hands, just as when we put our faith in God.
Testimony	• Allow people a chance to share their own testimonies about how God has delivered them or a loved one through a time of illness.

Sermon 💡 Boosters cont.

Booster	Idea
Video	• Show a clip from the movie, *What About Bob?* Use the section where Bob's psychiatrist introduces the idea of "baby steps" from his book. Explain that, at times, we need to take baby steps in our journey of faith, and that this is still a healthy way to overcome obstacles. Taking baby steps in your faith walk is better than standing still. • Show a video of the inner workings of an elevator. Explain that most of what makes the elevator run is behind the scenes and out of sight. So it is with faith. God is constantly at work in our lives "behind the scenes," developing our faith. • Show a clip from the film, *Ghandi Part I,* distributed by Columbia, 1982. (Start time: 16:52. End time: 19:18.) Ghandi and an English minister are threatened by racist youths. Ghandi quotes Jesus about turning the other cheek. This would be an effective illustration of faith coming from an unexpected source because the Hindu, not the Christian, quoted Jesus.
WOTS	• Videotape people in the community responding to the questions, "What is faith?" "When have you been surprised by God?" "Do you know anyone who has been miraculously healed?" "Has anyone ever let you down?" "What qualities do you look for in someone to trust?" • Videotape children's responses to the question, "When you need help, who do you go to?"

Stereotypes of Segregation

John 4:4–42

Now [Jesus] had to go through Samaria. So he came to a town in Samaria called Sychar, near the plot of ground Jacob had given to his son Joseph. Jacob's well was there, and Jesus, tired as he was from the journey, sat down by the well. It was about the sixth hour. When a Samaritan woman came to draw water, Jesus said to her, "Will you give me a drink?" (His disciples had gone into the town to buy food.)

The Samaritan woman said to him, "You are a Jew and I am a Samaritan woman. How can you ask me for a drink?" (For Jews do not associate with Samaritans.)

Jesus answered her, "If you knew the gift of God and who it is that asks you for a drink, you would have asked him and he would have given you living water."

"Sir," the woman said, "you have nothing to draw with and the well is deep. Where can you get this living water? Are you greater than our father Jacob, who gave us the well and drank from it himself, as did also his sons and his flocks and herds?"

Jesus answered, "Everyone who drinks this water will be thirsty again, but whoever drinks the water I give him will never thirst. Indeed, the water I give him will become in him a spring of water welling up to eternal life."

The woman said to him, "Sir, give me this water so that I won't get thirsty and have to keep coming here to draw water."

He told her, "Go, call your husband and come back."

"I have no husband," she replied.

Jesus said to her, "You are right when you say you have no husband. The fact is, you have had five husbands, and the man you now have is not your husband. What you have just said is quite true."

"Sir," the woman said, "I can see that you are a prophet. Our fathers worshiped on this mountain, but you Jews claim that the place where we must worship is in Jerusalem."

Jesus declared, "Believe me, woman, a time is coming when you will worship the Father neither on this mountain nor in Jerusalem. You Samaritans worship what you do not know; we worship what we do know, for salvation is from the Jews. Yet a time is coming and has now come when the true worshipers will worship the Father in spirit and truth, for they are the kind of worshipers the Father seeks. God is spirit, and his worshipers must worship in spirit and in truth."

The woman said, "I know that Messiah" (called Christ) "is coming. When he comes, he will explain everything to us." Then Jesus declared, "I who speak to you am he."

Just then his disciples returned and were surprised to find him talking with a woman. But no one asked, "What do you want?" or "Why are you talking with her?"

Then, leaving her water jar, the woman went back to the town and said to the people, "Come, see a man who told me everything I ever did. Could this be the Christ?" They came out of the town and made their way toward him.

Meanwhile his disciples urged him, "Rabbi, eat something." But he said to them, "I have food to eat that you know nothing about."

Then his disciples said to each other, "Could someone have brought him food?"

"My food," said Jesus, "is to do the will of him who sent me and to finish his work. Do you not say, 'Four months more and then the harvest'? I tell you, open your eyes and look at the fields! They are ripe for harvest. Even now the reaper draws his wages, even now he harvests the crop for eternal life, so that the sower and the reaper may be glad together. Thus the saying 'One sows and another reaps' is true. I sent you to reap what you have not worked for. Others have done the hard work, and you have reaped the benefits of their labor."

Many of the Samaritans from that town believed in him because of the woman's testimony, "He told me everything I ever did." So when the Samaritans came to him, they urged him to stay with them, and he stayed two days. And because of his words many more became believers. They said to the woman, "We no longer believe just because of what you said; now we have heard for ourselves, and we know that this man really is the Savior of the world."

Mood  Setters

Setting	Idea
Announcements	• Ask two people to give the announcements, each emphasizing how *their* announcement is just for *their* group, illustrating the concept of how we often stereotype according to "us" and "them." This should be done in a comical, exaggerated fashion. Choose two people of different genders and/or ages.
Building and Grounds	• Set up a replica of a well in front of the entrance to the church. You may also put up a sign indicating an area of your town or city that people are afraid to go to. For example, "The East Side Well."
Bulletin	• Print the bulletin in three or four different colors. Display poster board with the same colors in separate areas of the sanctuary. The ushers instruct the people to sit in the area of the sanctuary that corresponds with the color of their bulletin. Accompany this Mood Setter with the Introduction to the service explained below.
Communion	• Open the communion time with two people of obvious different economic status coming forward to receive the elements together. One is dressed in a business suit or dress with jewelry and the other is dressed in ragged jeans and has messed-up hair. • Serve communion using either marble rye or rainbow bread, illustrating the unity in the body of Christ. Only in Christ can we truly overcome the mentality of "us" versus "them."
Drama	• Ask four to six people to perform, *Them,* by Randy Petersen (available in script and on video). Characters include one man, three women, and two optional extras. The drama is set in a local grocery store. It pictures a struggle between good and evil that catapults a homemaker to break through her fears and prejudices. She is accompanied by an angel and a devil who battle to win the mind of this impressionable Christian.
Greeters and Ushers	• The greeters and ushers dress in different styles of clothing representing various social or economic classes. • The greeters and ushers on one side of the sanctuary wear dark-colored clothing while those on the other side wear light-colored clothing, indicating the concept of "us versus them."

Mood 🕯 Setters cont.

Setting	Idea
Introduction	• Near the beginning of the service, refer to how each person has been segregated according to his or her bulletin color. Point out that people have been asked to sit according to ways people often stereotype each other—size, gender, age, hair color, eye color, etc. Segregation by bulletin color is meant to show how uncomfortable it feels to have a stereotype unnaturally imposed upon people.
Performance Art	• Set up a tableau of the Lord's Supper. Several people dress to represent a variety of occupations. They take their place with Christ in frozen positions at the table.
Prelude	• Choose a hymn or chorus and play it in a variety of musical styles (such as pipe organ, symphony, big band, Beach Boys, rock and roll, hip hop, etc.). Point out that throughout the service, the music remained the same but the style changed. The same is true of us as well, although there are a number of different types of people, we must keep from judging and placing stereotypes on others. In the end, Jesus only cares about what our hearts look like.
Reading	• Ask someone to read the children's book, *The Sneeches*, by Dr. Seuss. You could have the reader sit in a chair surrounded by children. To include the rest of the congregation, show slides or scan the story illustrations on Power Point and project them on a screen above the children. • Read an excerpt from Philip Yancey's, *The Jesus I Never Knew,* published by Zondervan (pp. 153–154.) Yancey illustrates how Jesus turned the world upside down with his attitudes toward women and the oppressed.

Sermon 💡 Boosters

Booster	Idea
Application	• Insert a "Prayer Prompter" in the bulletin. Include an extensive list of areas in which people may be biased. Use this time of reflection to help the congregation identify their own prejudices. Then, invite them to write down a specific time during the upcoming week that they'll reach out to those they had previously considered "them."

Sermon 💡 Boosters cont.

Booster	Idea
Character	• If the pastor is female, she may dress as the Samaritan woman at the well and tell the story from her point of view.
Discussion Groups	• Break up into groups of four to six and discuss, "How do you overcome barriers of personal prejudice in order to bring others to Christ?" Point out that not only did Jesus accept the Samaritan woman, but he also showed her the way to the truth.
Dress	• The pastor dresses down for the day to illustrate how we can even impose stereotypes from something as simple as the way someone dresses. This is especially effective if he or she typically wears more formal clothing.
Interruption	• As the pastor is telling the story from John 4:4–42, have two or three people act as Samaritan townspeople who know the woman at the well. They interrupt the sermon by rushing in from the back of the sanctuary up to the front platform. With much excitement, they should explain to the pastor the scriptural story as if the event had just happened and Jesus was still out at the well.
	• A disciple rushes in as the pastor tells the story saying, "Wait a minute, why is Jesus talking to this woman? Doesn't he know what kind of a woman she is? And what's he talking about food for? He hasn't even eaten yet!"
Interview	• Interview someone who might have been considered a modern-day woman at the well. Consider someone who would be vulnerable in sharing her story openly. Focus the questions on how her life has radically turned around since she encountered Jesus.
	• Interview someone who has been an outcast and has been brought into the church community.
Movement	• The pastor enters from the back of the sanctuary as he/she begins the sermon, acting as if he/she is talking to the crowd of Samaritans who, after hearing the woman's testimony, returned to meet Jesus.
Panel Discussion	• Make up a panel of actors playing various townspeople and disciples who were eyewitnesses to Jesus' encounter with the Samaritan woman. You may even include her on the panel.

Sermon 💡 Boosters cont.

Booster	Idea
Prayer	• Break into groups and pray with someone who has a different bulletin color. (See Bulletin section above.) • Break into groups of four to five and pray for unity in your church and community. • The pastor leads the congregation in a time of guided prayer, helping people get past their personal stereotypes toward Christlike compassion.
WOTS	• Go into the community and videotape responses to the question, "Who do you have a hard time accepting?"

Thematic Service

Theme 8

Jesus Shattered the Stereotypes of "Us" and "Them"

Luke 18:9–24

PRELUDE

PRAISE AND WORSHIP 10 minutes

VIDEO 5 minutes

Show a clip from the film, *Godspell,* of Jesus telling the parable of the Pharisee and the tax collector.

WELCOME AND ANNOUNCEMENTS 6 minutes

Two people give the announcements in a "one-up-manship" style. Each one tries to outdo the other, borrowing from the Pharisee's attitude and dialogue. For example, after the first one gives an announcement, the second person says to the congregation, "Well, I'm glad I'm not like *that* person. *I'm* having my car washed by the youth next Saturday morning at 10:00. And *I'm* going to attend Bible study at 7:00 every Monday night this month."

OFFERING 3 minutes

DRAMA 5 minutes

"Them" (Randy Peterson, Mainstay Church Resources)*

SERMON 30 minutes

The pastor interviews the Pharisee and the tax collector.

SPECIAL MUSIC 5 minutes

"Whisper Heard Around the World" (Bryan Duncan on *Blue Skies,* Myrrh)

POSTLUDE

(Total Service Time **66 minutes**)

---

* To obtain these resources, see the resource section on page 186.

REMEMBER

- Adapt these services to fit your worship style. Choose the elements that will communicate best to your congregation.
- Don't mix metaphors when selecting service elements.
- Change the times for each element to suit your needs.
- Substitute music or dramatic elements to suit your setting.
- Think through the flow from element to element. Transitions can be as simple as a phrase or two by a worship leader or other service participant.

Additional Resources

Overall Topic: Stereotypes: Shattering Beliefs That Bind Us

Suggested Dramas

Drama Title	Author	Publisher
"Fruit Market Mayhem"	The Timberlakes	Mainstay Church Resources
"Them"	Randy Peterson	Mainstay Church Resources
"Sandbox Blues"	Tom Hutchison	Mainstay Church Resources
"The Dorm Room"	John Yarbrough	Mainstay Church Resources
"Another Day at the Bus Stop"	Judson Poling	Zondervan ChurchSource
"Half-baked"	Donna Lagerquist	Zondervan ChurchSource

Suggested Special Music

Song	Artist	Compact Disc	Label
"Believe It to See It"	Eric Champion	*Touch*	Brentwood
"Color Blind"	Michael W. Smith	*Change Your World*	Reunion
"Steps of Faith"	Bob Carlisle	*The Hope of a Man*	Sparrow
"From Love to Love"	Babbie Mason	*A World of Difference*	Word
"Colored People"	DC Talk	*Jesus Freak*	Aristomedia
"One Day Before Someday"	Jackson Finch	*Experience*	Warner
"Common Creed"	Wes King	*Common Creed*	Reunion
"Pretending"	Out of the Grey	*Gravity*	Sparrow
"That's Not Jesus"	Wayne Watson	*The Fine Line*	Warner Alliance
"Shake"	Russ Taff	*Russ Taff*	Word

Suggested Special Music, cont.

Song	Artist	Compact Disc	Label
"Whisper Heard Around the World"	Bryan Duncan	*Blue Skies*	Myrrh

Suggested Worship Songs

Song	Label
"Blest Are They"	G.I.A. Publications
"The Bond of Love"	Lillenas
"Change My Heart, O God"	Mercy Publications
"Glorify Thy Name in All the Earth"	Integrity Music
"Let the Walls Fall Down"	Maranatha
"More Love, More Power"	Vineyard
"Prayer of St. Francis"	Franciscan Communications Center
"Show Me Your Ways"	Hillsong/Australia
"They'll Know We Are Christians"	F.E.L. Pub.
"We Will Stand"	Myrrh

CHAPTER FIVE

Encouragement: Drawing Out the Best in Others

Theme 9

Encouraging the Afflicted–Mark 5:1–20

Related Topics: demon possession, identity of Christ, acceptance in Christ, power of Christ, freedom in Christ, evangelism, new life in Christ

Theme 10

Encouraging the Outsider—Luke 19:1–10

Related Topics: Zacchaeus, salvation, Son of Man, grace, love of Christ, acceptance in Christ, evangelism, new life in Christ

Theme 11

Encouraging the Young—Mark 10:13–16

Related Topics: children, acceptance in Christ, kingdom of God, mentoring, childlike faith, obstacles to faith, child dedication

Theme 12

Thematic Service

Jesus Liked People and Drew Out the Best in Them—Luke 19:1–10

Related Topics: Zacchaeus, salvation, Son of Man, grace, love of Christ, acceptance in Christ, evangelism, new life in Christ

Theme 9

Encouraging the Afflicted

Mark 5:1–20

They went across the lake to the region of the Gerasenes. When Jesus got out of the boat, a man with an evil spirit came from the tombs to meet him. This man lived in the tombs, and no one could bind him any more, not even with a chain. For he had often been chained hand and foot, but he tore the chains apart and broke the irons on his feet. No one was strong enough to subdue him. Night and day among the tombs and in the hills he would cry out and cut himself with stones.

When he saw Jesus from a distance, he ran and fell on his knees in front of him. He shouted at the top of his voice, "What do you want with me, Jesus, Son of the Most High God? Swear to God that you won't torture me!" For Jesus had said to him, "Come out of this man, you evil spirit!"

Then Jesus asked him, "What is your name?"

"My name is Legion," he replied, "for we are many." And he begged Jesus again and again not to send them out of the area.

A large herd of pigs was feeding on the nearby hillside. The demons begged Jesus, "Send us among the pigs; allow us to go into them." He gave them permission, and the evil spirits came out and went into the pigs. The herd, about two thousand in number, rushed down the steep bank into the lake and were drowned.

Those tending the pigs ran off and reported this in the town and countryside, and the people went out to see what had happened. When they came to Jesus, they saw the man who had been possessed by the legion of demons, sitting there, dressed and in his right mind; and they were afraid. Those who had seen it told the people what had happened to the demon-possessed man—and told about the pigs as well. Then the people began to plead with Jesus to leave their region.

As Jesus was getting into the boat, the man who had been demon-possessed begged to go with him. Jesus did not let him, but said, "Go home to your family and tell them how much the Lord has done for you, and how he has had mercy on you." So the man went away and began to tell in the Decapolis how much Jesus had done for him. And all the people were amazed.

Mood  Setters

Setting	Idea
Announcements	• The person giving the announcements wears a pig nose to represent a pig from the passage. (Your congregation won't sleep through these announcements!)
	• If using the radio show idea (see Introduction below), do the announcements as though they were a commercial in the radio show. Use the announcer from the radio show to give the church announcements.
	• Create a skit that illustrates what it's like when everyone but one person is chosen for a team. Have a predetermined number of people come up to the front to help give announcements. Someone should act like the team captain. Have this person pick one volunteer at a time to help read the announcements. Each time the captain picks someone for the team, everyone can call out things like, "Ooh, ooh, pick me! Pick me!" Finally, the announcement team is chosen leaving one

Mood  Setters cont.

Setting	Idea
Announcements, cont.	not chosen. Once the announcements are given, everyone exits the platform while the one who wasn't chosen remains. This person should act hurt and dejected by what has just taken place. The pastor enters and gives this person a warm embrace. Then, in order to set up the theme of the service, have them talk together about how it feels to be unwanted.
Application	• Hand out links of chains to remind the congregation that Jesus has broken the power of sin and the chains that bind us to it.
Building and Grounds	• Someone dressed as a homeless person stands outside the entrance of your church building holding a construction paper sign that reads, "Will work for food." Perhaps this homeless person could even interact with those entering church—begging for money, asking for food, etc. During the welcome and greeting, ask the congregation if they felt uncomfortable when they approached the building. Explain that even when we feel awkward around certain people, we are called to follow Christ's example: he liked all people and knew how to bring out the best in everyone. • Construct a pigpen outside the front of the church entrance. Have a local farmer bring a number of swine to place in it. Use this as a way of introducing the Scripture passage for the day.
Communion	• Set up an open microphone during the communion time for people to share a testimony. Ask them to consider what their response would be if Jesus told them to tell their friends, "Look what the Lord has done for me." • As people come forward to receive the communion elements, also give them a link from a chain. Tell each one that this is a reminder that they have been set free from the sin that binds and chains them.
Drama	• Ask three people to perform *In a Pig's Eye,* by Doug and Melissa Timberlake (available in script and on video). Three pigs from a nearby herd discuss a peculiar visit to their rowdy neighbor, the demoniac. A famous prophet, named Jesus, has decided to stop by. These rambunctious and hilarious swine characters contemplate the actions of this odd rabbi who seems to like all people and even brings out the best in them.
Greeters and Ushers	• When the greeters and ushers hand people bulletins, they also give each person a key. During the welcome and greeting,

Mood 🕯 Setters cont.

Setting	Idea

Greeters and Ushers, cont. explain that the keys are visual reminders of how Jesus freed the man in the Scripture passage from his bondage. Invite the congregation to take their keys home as personal reminders that Christ also loves each one of them and wants only the best for them—to free them from their sin.

Introduction

- Invite a team of Christian power lifters to give a brief demonstration for the introduction to the service. Then ask them to compare their power over physical objects with the power of God over all things, including spiritual bondage.
- Tell the story of the passage in a '40s radio show style. Set the mood with the theme music from the radio show "Unshackled" or other melodramatic organ music. Use an announcer to introduce the story and cue the players. Players form a semicircle around a microphone and hold their scripts as they tell the story. Set a sound effects booth to the side of the platform with a couple of people making the accompanying sounds like the chains rattling, people walking, the pigs running, water splashing, etc. The actors play all the parts in the scene, including the crowd and pigs.

Lighting

- As the congregation enters the sanctuary, place the lighting at a dim setting with just enough light to seat people. Use this darkness to set a mood of seriousness, visually representing the heaviness we feel when we have not been set free by Christ. At an appropriate time during the service or sermon, bring the lighting up completely. Let this lighting enhance a joyous celebration of the fact that Jesus loves us enough to set us free from bondage.

Performance Art

- Build a replica of a cage and cast someone to play the part of a person not in his right mind locked in the cage. Put a large padlock on it. The person inside should pace about, pull his hair, mumble, and rattle the cage. At the end of the service, this same person is neatly dressed and in his right mind. The door to the cage has been unlocked and the person is sitting calmly outside the cage. As people pass by, he says to them, "Look what the Lord has done for me."

Reading

- Read an excerpt from *Stories for the Heart* by Paul Brand (with Philip Yancey) titled "Belongings" (published by QuestarPublications, pp. 23–25). The story is about a leper whose life changes when he meets Jesus.

Mood ⓘ Setters cont.

Setting	Idea
Video	• Show the excerpt of the demon-possessed man from the Curt Cloninger video, *Witnesses*, produced by Gospel Films. This is a dramatic portrayal of the passage. • Show a clip from the film, *The Elephant Man* (EMI, 1980). John Merrick is being chased by a crowd and cries out, "I'm not an animal! I'm a human being." (Start time: 1:42:01. End time: 1:45:20.)
Visual Art	• Create a mural of many different types of chains and padlocks. Use the back wall behind the podium for display. Sometime before the sermon, have someone refer to the mural. Explain that sin causes us to be in bondage. Jesus' love is the key that breaks open the locks and chains that bind. • Create a backdrop for the back wall of the platform. Cut two large hearts from red construction paper or felt. Chains bind one heart and the other is unbound with the chains lying on the floor beneath the heart. The placement of the chains indicates the state of the heart. • Set a large cross on the platform or in the lobby. Surround the base of the cross with broken, discarded pieces of chains. Display a sign nearby that reads, "See what the Lord has done and how he has had mercy on you."

Sermon 🔅 Boosters

Booster	Idea
Action Step	• Challenge your people to take today's lesson and put feet to their faith by helping out at an area soup kitchen, or some other place where they can be an encouragement through volunteering. • Give people the opportunity to write down an area of their lives that feels unlovable. Once everyone has had sufficient time to think this through and write down something specific, have a time of prayer to ask Jesus to break the lie that some areas of our lives are unlovable. Next, have everyone stand and tear their cards to shreds as a symbolic way of reemphasizing the fact that Jesus truly does love us even the areas of our lives that seem unlovable.

Sermon Boosters cont.

Booster	Idea
Discussion Groups	• Divide the congregation into groups of five to seven and discuss how they've experienced Jesus' divine love.
Interruption	• A farmer from your congregation, or someone dressed like a farmer, stands and is angry that Jesus destroyed all of his pigs. "Those pigs were worth a lot of money!" he hollers. "Who's going to replace my pigs? I want an explanation!"
	• The pastor begins the sermon with a very deadpan reading of the passage. A few sentences into the passage he/she is interrupted by someone speaking from the point of view of the man Jesus encountered. He runs up to the platform and says, "No, it was much more spectacular than that—let me tell you what happened to me," and continues the story in the first person, excited about what the Lord did for him.
Interview	• Interview a person from the congregation whose life was completely out of control before he/she met Jesus. Ask him/her to share how his/her life has changed. This could be someone who has struggled with emotional illness or an addiction, etc.
	• Interview the director of a rescue mission or someone from the Salvation Army who has ministered to those who are outcast in our society. Ask them to share the life change that occurs when someone is shown unconditional love.
Object Lesson	• The pastor begins the sermon wearing a pair of handcuffs. At some point in the sermon have a police officer from the congregation, dressed in his uniform, come up and remove the handcuffs. Use this illustration to help show the point that, like the officer, Jesus has the authority to free us from whatever is holding us back from living for him.
Panel Discussion	• Gather a group of people who will be willing to talk about the struggles they've overcome with the help of Jesus. Have them focus on the fact that alone they couldn't beat the areas that were plaguing their lives. Only through the power of Jesus have they changed. Jesus is the One who is able to bring out the best in them. Have them also explain that even though they may have given up on themselves and felt unworthy at times, Jesus never did. Your panel could consist of people who have overcome such addictions as gambling, drugs, excessive shopping, materialism, etc.

Sermon (💡) Boosters cont.

Booster	Idea
Panel Discussion, cont.	• As a take-off on the movie, *Babe,* have a few people dressed as pigs taking part in a panel discussion about the madman who lived in their area. They would talk about what they saw and heard "on the day their cousins went over the cliff and drowned." • Gather a panel of people who have felt rejected or ostracized at some point in their life. This panel may include such people as those who are homeless, handicapped, gay, divorced and/or those who have struggled with emotional illness, addiction, racism, ageism or gender bias. Ask them to share where they are in the process of healing and how the church has participated in that healing.
Prayer	• Give people time to offer their areas of hurt and rejection to the Lord. After people have had time to pray about their own concerns, ask them to also lift up silent prayers for others they know who are suffering with feelings of being unloved, misunderstood, or outcast.
Reading	• Read an excerpt from *The Jesus I Never Knew Study Guide,* by Phillip Yancey/Brenda Quinn, published by Zondervan (pp. 78–79). The reading discusses the value Jesus places on "nobodies."
WOTS	• Go into the community and videotape people's responses to the statement "Tell me about a time you felt accepted by someone."

Theme 10

Encouraging the Outsider

Luke 19:1–10

Jesus entered Jericho and was passing through. A man was there by the name of Zacchaeus; he was a chief tax collector and was wealthy. He wanted to see who Jesus was, but being a short man he could not, because of the crowd. So he ran ahead and climbed a sycamore-fig tree to see him, since Jesus was coming that way.

When Jesus reached the spot, he looked up and said to him, "Zacchaeus, come down immediately. I must stay at your house today." So he came down at once and welcomed him gladly.

All the people saw this and began to mutter, "He has gone to be the guest of a 'sinner.'"

But Zacchaeus stood up and said to the Lord, "Look, Lord! Here and now I give half of my possessions to the poor, and if I have cheated anybody out of anything, I will pay back four times the amount."

Jesus said to him, "Today salvation has come to this house, because this man, too, is a son of Abraham. For the Son of Man came to seek and to save what was lost."

Mood Setters

Setting	Idea
Announcements	• A person gives the announcements dressed up as Zacchaeus.
Building and Grounds	• Near the front entrance of your church someone can be sitting in a tree. This person should be wearing a hat with the letters IRS printed on the front. If people ask what he's doing in the tree, have him respond, "I'm waiting for Jesus to arrive. I got up here so I could see over the huge crowd that always follows Jesus." • Hang a banner at the entrance to the church that reads, "Jesus came to seek and to save what was lost." • Set up an area on the grounds or in the lobby for an artist from the congregation to draw caricatures. Place a sign near the area that reads, "Drawing Out the Best." Make sure the artist exaggerates the person's *best* feature. For example, if the person is a great visionary, enhance the eyes; if someone exhibits a heart for God, focus on his heart; or if someone is a diligent servant, enlarge her hands. Give these drawings away—to be taken home as illustrations and reminders that Jesus draws out the best in people.
Communion	• During communion, a slide show runs showing the faces of many different people from different backgrounds and cultures. • During communion, give each participant a leaf from a tree to remind them of the extreme measure Zacchaeus went to in order to see Jesus.

Mood $\textbf{i}$ Setters cont.

Setting	Idea
Greeters and Ushers	• Zacchaeus went to the extreme to see Jesus. Have your greeters and ushers go to the extreme to convey that Jesus likes all people and will do anything to bring out the best in them. You might have your greeters and ushers meet people when they park. They could open the car doors for them and volunteer to escort them to the front of the church. Whatever it takes! Perhaps this would be a good week to incorporate the youth as greeters and ushers.
Introduction	• Someone who has been the recipient of love, acceptance, and grace extended in the name of Christ should share his/her experience. Ask this person to explain how this changed his/her life. Parallel those changes to the way Zacchaeus's life was changed.
Lobby	• Set up an area in the lobby to highlight service opportunities. During the service, encourage people to choose one of the many ways they can volunteer in helping reach out to the outcasts in the community. Examples of service opportunities might include Crisis Pregnancy Centers, Habitat for Humanity, Community Shelter Programs, etc.
Offering	• Take up a special offering for people or families who are in need or in a time of crisis. Ask your congregation to follow Zacchaeus's example by choosing to be extreme in their giving. By giving generously to these people in need, the church will help them feel loved and embraced at a time when they may be feeling misplaced.
	• After the message, invite people to consider Zacchaeus's extreme response to Jesus reaching out to him. Not only did he want to repay those he'd wronged, but he wanted to give many times more! Encourage people to consider Jesus' work in their lives and follow this "extreme" response as they participate in the offering that day.
Performance Art	• Cast someone to play the part of a contemporary counterpart to Zacchaeus, someone who is not generally accepted in our society (a homeless person or a gang member). This person simply hangs around the entrance to the building as people are coming in for the service. In either the sermon or as an introduction to the service, reveal that this was a planned event. Ask the congregation to consider what their feelings were as they encountered this person. Did they feel this person didn't

Mood (i) Setters cont.

Setting	Idea
Performance Art, cont.	belong at their church? Or did they respond as Jesus responded to Zacchaeus by acknowledging and welcoming him?
Prelude	• Open the service with the children's choir singing, "Zacchaeus Was a Wee Little Man."
Visual Art	• An artist in your church could construct a large tree out of paper to be displayed either in the lobby or on the wall behind the pulpit.
Welcome	• In order to set up the story of Zacchaeus, someone who is dressed as a stereotypical IRS agent could give the welcome. This person could wear a dark suit or dress, carry a briefcase marked IRS in large letters, and wear a button that also reads IRS.

Sermon (💡) Boosters

Booster	Idea
Action Step	• Prepare an insert or a place in the bulletin where people can write down the name of someone to whom they can reach out. Give the congregation time to write down a specific name. The pastor can then pray that God would give each one the strength and wisdom to know how to best begin reaching out to those people.
	• Create a list of possible ways to reach out to people who might relate to feeling like outsiders. Have a check box next to each idea. Ask the congregation to check the ideas that they are committing to try in the upcoming week.
	• In order to model to others that Jesus likes people, ask the congregation to make it a goal to give out at least five compliments this week.
Character	• Wear a Bible times outfit and preach from the perspective of Zacchaeus.
Discussion Groups	• Ask the congregation to break into discussion groups of four or five people to describe someone who has drawn out the best in them.

Sermon Boosters cont.

Booster	Idea
Environment	• Arrange an area of the platform to resemble a tax office such as H & R Block. Seat someone working at the desk and place a large nameplate on it that reads "Zacchaeus." At the close of the sermon, the pastor walks to the desk and invites "Zacchaeus" to go to lunch after the service.
Interruption	• Different people who are plants in the audience stand and complain about seeing Jesus with sinners. You might even use modern-day examples such as, "I saw Jesus sitting in a bar and talking to a drunk! Is that any way for a Savior to be acting?"
Panel Discussion	• Gather a group of people who can talk about the practical ways they've been able to connect with everyday people (such as a grocery clerk, gas station attendant, mailman, etc.). Ask them to also give examples of how they've been able to share the love of Jesus with those people.
Storytelling	• Tell the story of the *Velveteen Rabbit*. Relate how it had appeared to the characters in the story that the rabbit was worthless. But the Velveteen Rabbit was loved—making him a precious creation. Parallel the ideas in this story to the fact that we are all loved by Jesus. He is able to draw out the best in us—even when those around us treat us as worthless and unimportant.
Video	• Produce a video at a local soup kitchen or shelter where your church is getting involved. Be sure to have action shots of people from your congregation actually making a difference there. This will be an encouragement to the congregation while also dispersing some of the fears they may have of getting involved in a setting that's unfamiliar. • Use a video clip from the movie *The Elephant Man,* available from EMI, 1980. This clip should show how the doctor character reached out to someone who was unaccepted. Point out that the doctor drew out the best in the "elephant man." Because of the doctor's encouragement, his life was changed.
WOTS	• Ask people to describe someone who has drawn out the best in them. • Videotape the children of the congregation responding to the question, "What was a time you felt left out?"

Theme 11

Encouraging the Young

Mark 10:13–16

People were bringing little children to Jesus to have him touch them, but the disciples rebuked them. When Jesus saw this, he was indignant. He said to them, "Let the little children come to me, and do not hinder them, for the kingdom of God belongs to such as these. I tell you the truth, anyone who will not receive the kingdom of God like a little child will never enter it." And he took the children in his arms, put his hands on them and blessed them.

Mood Setters

Setting	Idea
Application	• Institute a mentoring program for children. In this program, older children may help younger children in Sunday school or another setting. Older children may also be asked to join teams as apprentices (such as assisting the technical or visual arts teams in some small way).
Building and Grounds	• Set oversized furniture outside the church on the lawn. Adults dressed as children sit on the furniture, emphasizing our need to become like little children. • If your service focuses on barriers to becoming childlike, set up a maze of obstacles (orange cones, a ladder, large garbage pails) along the walkway into the building. These obstacles will need to be placed so that people must walk around them in order to enter the building. Print specific barriers on strips of cardboard and attach them to the tops of the obstacles (pride, fear, embarrassment, overwork, too tired, etc.).
Child Dedication	• This is the perfect service to have a children's dedication. Include a reading of the Mark 10 passage and other selected Scripture verses that refer to our relationship with God the Father. Use the unexpected moments that happen with children during the dedication to enhance the theme of the service. For example, if a sibling of the child being dedicated tugs at a parent's sleeve for attention, rather than tell the child to behave, include him/her. Ask the child to tell why they love Jesus, or why Jesus loves children, etc.
Greeters	• Partner children with adults to act as greeters. • Greeters dress as children, welcoming people into the service.
Handout	• Pass out balloons as people leave the sanctuary to remind them to be like little children.

Mood (i) Setters cont.

Setting	Idea
Introduction	• The person doing the introduction to the service talks about how we need to accept children and take time for them. A child runs in and interrupts, tugging on the adult's arm. The adult tells the child, "Wait a minute! Wait a minute!" and shoos the child away. There should be an obvious contrast between what the adult says and does. • An adult and a child do the introduction to the service together. The child appears to be shy, awkward, and uncomfortable. The adult verbally encourages him, attempting to help him feel more comfortable. The child then begins to smile and put aside some of his shyness. Soon, the two are dialoging the announcements back and forth and having fun doing it! Somewhere in the middle of the announcements, have the adult explain that sometimes even big people feel shy and frightened. At those times, it is important to remember that Jesus likes all of us and wants to draw out the best in us.
Lobby	• A week or two before this Sunday, have the children in Sunday school draw pictures illustrating their responses to the question, "What does Jesus like about me?" Display their artwork in a children's art gallery in the lobby. Title the gallery, "What Jesus Likes About Me." • Display photographs in the lobby of your church leaders as children. Number each photo. List the numbers on a bulletin insert with the names out of order. People can try to match the photos with the correct names. • Display photographs in the lobby of heroes of the faith when they were children (Billy Graham, Dwight L. Moody). Later in the service, refer to these photos, pointing out how children need our encouragement to become the best they can be because we never know what God may call them to do.
Performance Art	• A group of children dressed in Bible time garb sit in a circle on the lawn in front of the church. A man, also dressed in Bible time garb, acts as Jesus and teaches the children. • Someone acts as a Pied Piper, leading the children in a game of "Follow the Leader." The youngsters should be having fun, giggling, following, and singing. Have them carry little flags with "Jesus Likes Me" written on them. The person playing the Pied Piper should call out the phrase in a sing-song fashion, "Unless you become like a child, you will not enter the kingdom of heaven." This verse should then be repeated back to the Pied Piper by the children.

Mood  Setters cont.

Setting	Idea
Prelude/Transition Music	• Use the song "Jesus Loves Me" with an upbeat, jazzy feel, at three-quarter time. Also use it as instrumental transition music throughout the service, in a variety of appropriate styles. Close the service with it as a congregational song, reminding people that Jesus told us that unless we become like little children, we won't enter the kingdom of God.
Sound Effects	• Play a tape in the lobby of children laughing. This can be particularly effective if the children's art gallery is also in the lobby.
Transition	• Tape a voice-over of children giving their testimonies. Play the tape as a transition from one element to the next throughout the service. • Play a tape of children laughing as a transition throughout the service.
Video	• Show a clip from a "Veggie Tales" video about Jesus loving us.

Sermon ☀ Boosters

Booster	Idea
Action Step	• Walk the congregation through practical ways to discover answers to the question, "How does Jesus want me to become more childlike?" Use a dialogue format in which two people go back and forth explaining what to do and what not to do in this discovery exercise. For example, "*Do* look for ways to have a simple faith. *Don't* look for simple things to have faith about." • Explain the concept of "sacred play" as the quality of childlike rejoicing and celebrating in a worshiplike activity before God. (See *Sacred Play*, Wenda Shereos, Mainstay Church Resources, p. 26.) Ask the congregation to give themselves permission to enter into "sacred play" once a week for the next month. Schedule a time during an upcoming worship service for people to share how their relationship with God has been effected through their experiences. • Refer to pages 59 and 74 in the book, *Sacred Play*, by Wenda Shereos (Mainstay Church Resources). Select one or two of the

Sermon ☺ Boosters cont.

Booster	Idea
Action Step, cont.	practical exercises at the end of the chapters to use as applications to the message.
Application	• An elder in the church washes the feet of a child in a foot-washing ceremony. This action models the loving attitude Jesus had and the importance he placed on children.
Cartoon	• Show a cartoon of a father and son. In one frame, the son is kneeling at his bedside and prays, "God, please make me more like Daddy." In the next frame, the father kneels at his bedside and prays, "God, please make me more like my son." You may show the cartoon on an overhead transparency, a slide, Power Point, or as a bulletin insert. • Using software that turns photos into cartoons, insert pictures of members of the congregation. Use these as an example of delighting in having fun.
Character	• The pastor preaches from the viewpoint of the disciple Mark. (It has been conjectured that perhaps Mark was one of the children that Jesus took into his arms and blessed in this passage.)
Discussion Groups	• Break the congregation up into groups of three to five people. Ask them to discuss their answers to the question, "What barriers do you have to overcome in becoming more childlike in your relationship with Jesus?"
Environment	• The pastor preaches in an environment made up of really large furniture. He/she may even get into an oversized chair or couch. • The pastor preaches in an environment set up to look like a child's room.
Interruption	• A child interrupts the pastor in the middle of the sermon, entering onto the platform and tugging on the pastor's jacket. An adult stands up in the congregation and reprimands the child for interrupting. The pastor responds as Jesus would, welcoming the child and his/her questions.
Interview	• Interview a Sunday school teacher about the qualities he/she has observed in children that we as adults need to adopt in order to become more childlike in our relationship with God.

Sermon 💡 Boosters cont.

Booster	Idea
Interview, cont.	Interview someone about a Sunday school teacher who impacted his/her life.
Object Lesson	• The pastor invites a child to join him/her in doing an object lesson. • Hand out simple awards to the children of the congregation as a lesson in encouraging children and bringing out the best in them.
Panel Discussion	• The pastor moderates a panel made up of children ages five through eight. Use a format like the television show, "Kids Say the Darndest Things." Ask the children to answer, "What makes you feel important?" • Bring together a panel of people from the congregation who came to know Christ as adults. Discuss ways in which they had to become as little children when they received Christ. Discuss the challenge we face as adults to remain childlike in our relationship to our heavenly Father.
Reading	• Read an excerpt from the book *Sacred Play* by Wenda Shereos (pp. 19 and 26) as an introduction to the sermon. Available through Mainstay Church Resources.
Storytelling	• Invite the children to sit on the floor of the platform as an illustration of Jesus teaching the children. Ask several to act out a parable as the pastor reads it from the Bible.
Video	• Show the music video, *Life Is Precious*, by Wes King. The video features children performing in a small theater. • Show a clip from the *Jesus* video that illustrates this passage.
WOTS	• Show a video of kids responding to the question, "What does Jesus like about you?"

Thematic Service

Theme 12

Jesus Liked People and Drew Out the Best in Them

Luke 19:1–10

Mood  Setter

Set up an area on the grounds or in the lobby for an artist from the congregation to draw caricatures. Place a sign near the area that reads "Drawing Out the Best." Make sure the artist exaggerates the person's *best* feature. For example, if the person is a great visionary, enhance his eyes; if she exhibits a heart for God, focus on her heart; or if he is a diligent servant, enlarge his hands. Give the drawing to them to take home as an illustration and remembrance that Jesus draws out the best in people.

PRELUDE

Open the service with the children's choir singing, "Zacchaeus Was a Wee Little Man."

DRAMA 6 minutes

"In a Pig's Eye" (Doug and Melissa Timberlake, Mainstay Church Resources)*

WELCOME 2 minutes

PRAISE AND WORSHIP 12 minutes

ANNOUNCEMENTS AND OFFERING 5 minutes

Display the announcements using Power Point while the offering is being taken.

SPECIAL MUSIC 5 minutes

"Second String" (Wes King on *The Robe*, Reunion)

SERMON 30 minutes

Tell the story of the *Velveteen Rabbit*. Relate how it had appeared to everyone that the rabbit was worthless, but when loved, was a precious creation. When we are loved by Jesus, he draws out the best in us.

SPECIAL MUSIC 5 minutes

"Treasure of You" (Stephen Curtis Chapman on *Heaven in a Real World*)

POSTLUDE

(Total Service Time **67 minutes**)

---

* To obtain these resources, see the resource section on page 186.

REMEMBER

- Adapt these services to fit your worship style. Choose the elements that will communicate best to your congregation.
- Don't mix metaphors when selecting service elements.
- Change the times for each element to suit your needs.
- Substitute music or dramatic elements to suit your setting.
- Think through the flow from element to element. Transitions can be as simple as a phrase or two by a worship leader or other service participant.

Additional Resources

Overall Topic: Encouragement: Drawing Out the Best in Others

Suggested Dramas

Drama Title	Author	Publisher
"In a Pig's Eye"	The Timberlakes	Mainstay Church Resources
"And a Child Shall Lead Them"	Lynn Wilson	Mainstay Church Resources
"Funny Girl"	Donna Lagerquist	Zondervan ChurchSource
"You Matter to God"	Deb Poling	Zondervan ChurchSource
"Living for Them"	Tom Cox	Creative ResourceGroup

Suggested Special Music

Song	Artist	Compact Disc	Label
"Remember Your Chains"	Stephen Curtis Chapman	Heaven in the Real Word	Sparrow
"Mystery"	John Cox	Sunny Day	Questar
"That's How Much I Love You"	Kathy Troccoli	Sounds of Heaven	Reunion
"Picture Perfect"	Michael W. Smith	Change Your World	Reunion
"No One Knows My Heart"	Susan Ashton	Wakened by the Wind	Sparrow
"In Heaven's Eyes"	Sandi Patti	Make His Praise Glorious	Word
"Second String"	Wes King	The Robe	Reunion
"Place in This World"	Michael W. Smith	Go West Young Man	Reunion
"Treasure of You"	Stephen Curtis Chapman	Heaven in a Real World	Sparrow

Suggested Special Music, cont.

Song	Artist	Compact Disc	Label
"For Always"	BeBe and CeCe Winans	*Greatest Hits*	Sparrow
"God Help the Outcast"		Soundtrack for *The Hunchback of Notre Dame*	Walt Disney

Suggested Worship Songs

Song	Compact Disc or Book
"As We Gather"	*Integrity Book I*
"Honor and Praise"	*Integrity Book I*
"Lord Most High"	*Integrity Book XI*
"We Bring the Sacrifice of Praise"	*Integrity Book I*
"We Will Glorify"	*Integrity Book I*
"Bind Us Together"	*Thank You Music*
"We Believe in God"	*Songs from the Loft*
"Hey Now"	*Songs from the Loft*
"We Are His Hands"	*Bug 'n Bear Music*

CHAPTER SIX

Humility:
Serving As Jesus Did

Theme 13

Serving with Humility—Luke 22:24–30

Related Topics: *foot washing, acts of service, servant's heart, servant evangelism, greatness*

Theme 14

Serving: Shining Jesus' Light—John 1:1–18

Related Topics: *the Word, witnessing to the Light, Light of the World, Bread of Life, John the Baptist*

Theme 15

Serving with Honor—Luke 14:1–14

Related Topics: *healing, Pharisees, Sabbath, parable*

Theme 16

Thematic Service

Jesus Knew His Identity Yet Served with Humility—Luke 22:24–30

Related Topics: *acts of service, servant's heart, servant evangelism, greatness*

Theme 13

Serving with Humility

Luke 22:24–30

Also a dispute arose among them as to which of them was considered to be greatest. Jesus said to them, "The kings of the Gentiles lord it over them; and those who exercise authority over them call themselves Benefactors. But you are not to be like that. Instead, the greatest among you should be like the youngest, and the one who rules like the one who serves. For who is greater, the one who is at the table or the one who serves? Is it not the one who is at the table? But I am among you as one who serves. You are those who have stood by me in my trials. And I confer on you a kingdom, just as my Father conferred one on me, so that you may eat and drink at my table in my kingdom and sit on thrones, judging the twelve tribes of Israel."

Mood Setters

Setting	Idea
Announcements	• In order to help people focus on the part of the Luke 22 passage which reads, "Who is greater, the one who is at the table or the one who serves?" the person giving the announcements is dressed as a waiter. He/she should be carrying a large folder designed to look like a menu and read each announcement as if it were a selection from the menu. For example, "Today's appetizers include the Senior High Lock-In and the Junior High Skate Night on Monday. Our main courses include the Wednesday Night Prayer and Share and our Outreach Class beginning on Friday nights. And for dessert, who could resist the scrumptious Comedy Café next Sunday night, complete with ice cream and cookies?"
Building and Grounds	• As people walk up to the church, they see a group of people standing outside arguing with one another. When they get closer, they might even hear that the argument is over which one of them will be the greatest in the kingdom of God. • The leadership team is assembled at the front of the church prepared to valet park for those who want to use this "one day service." A sign at the parking lot entrance informs people that today the leadership team is offering an optional valet parking service.
Bulletin	• Design the bulletin to look like a menu. • Provide Service Opportunity Cards in the bulletin. List areas for people to serve in the church. Examples would include hospitality, visitation, care for the building and grounds, work with the children, volunteering in the office, etc.

Mood 🕯 Setters cont.

Setting	Idea
Communion	• Invite young people to participate in serving the communion elements. As the elements are being distributed, challenge the congregation to consider what Jesus meant when he said, "The greatest among you should be like the youngest, and the one who rules like the one who serves."
Drama	• Ask three people to perform *The Interview* by Joel Mains (available in script and on video). An interview for a high profile vice president position takes an unexpected turn as the applicant finds himself waiting in the supply room. The janitor, mistaking him for his new assistant, attempts to put him to work. A confrontation ensues and the outcome is a lesson in humility.
Environment	• Place twelve ornate chairs on the platform. Each should have a sign that reads "Reserved Seating." • Use the following items to create an environment on the sanctuary platform: a dressing stand, a towel and basin, a crown of thorns, a serving cart with serving platter. These items can be later referenced in the sermon as visual ways to help bring the passage to life.
Greeters and Ushers	• Dress the greeters in T-shirts from the "Veggie Tales" series that feature Bob the Tomato's picture and the caption, "How can I help you?" The ushers could wear buttons with the same picture and phrase written on them. • To emphasize the theme of serving, dress your greeters and ushers in different types of service uniforms.
Handout	• Give each person a small piece of towel as they leave as a reminder that we should have an attitude of service. • Give each person a pin that reads "How can I help you?" and a picture of Bob the Tomato on it. These can be found in most Christian bookstores. As an alternative, use a computer to design a replica of the buttons and run them off on labels or stickers.
Lobby	• People dressed as butlers and maids are offering orange juice or some small treat. They should be very courteous and proper.
Offering	• Provide envelopes for the offering labeled "My act of service." Remind the congregation that we do not give to get, but that

Mood 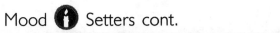 Setters cont.

Setting	Idea
Offering, cont.	giving is an act of service. Invite the people to enclose their offering in the envelope as an intentional act of service that morning.
Performance Art	• Before the service begins, stage a very simple scene on the platform of Jesus washing the disciples' feet. Light the scene so that all participants appear in silhouette. You may choose to keep this tableau for the whole service, or allow the participants to exit at an appropriate transition in the service.
Prelude/Performance Art	• Play the song "The Basin and the Towel." • One musician begins playing the prelude on the keyboard. Another musician enters from the back of the sanctuary muttering loud enough to be heard by the congregation, "I should be playing this number. I've studied longer. I don't know who picked this piece, and for that matter why they didn't ask me to play, everyone knows I'm the best!" He/she then walks up to the keyboardist and insists on showing how it should be done. The first musician objects and the pastor walks to the platform and says, "Jesus had some words that would be appropriate right about now," and opens the service by reading Luke 22:24–30.
Video	• Show a clip from the *Jesus* video of the scene where Jesus serves at the table. • Show the music video *Love You With My Life* by Stephen Curtis Chapman, distributed by Sparrow.
Visual Art	• Set a basin and towel on the platform as a visual reminder of Jesus' servant heart when he washed the disciples' feet.
Welcome	• Someone acting as a maître d' is dressed in a tuxedo. Place him to the side of the platform behind a podium with a welcome sign next to it. This person should be very elegant in his speech and grandiose in his desire to make sure everyone knows that they are welcome and special this morning. • After the pastor has welcomed the congregation, invite a child up to the platform. Remind the people that Jesus said, "The greatest among you should be like the youngest." The child then reads the passage from a children's translation of the Bible.

Sermon  Boosters

Booster	Idea
Application	• Ask the congregation to consider a ministry area or person they will serve this week. Have them fill in their response on an insert in the bulletin that reads, "This week I will serve _____."
	• Ask your church whether they want to be a full-service church or a self-service church, using a play on gas station protocol. Explain that a full-service church is one that rushes out to meet the needs of the people in the community. A self-service church says, "Do it on your own. We're too busy."
Cartoon	• Pull a still from a "VeggieTales" video of Bob the Tomato asking, "How can I help you?" and project it on a screen or insert it in the bulletin to give people a visual reminder to be servants that week.
Discussion Groups	• Give your congregation roughly three minutes to get into groups of three to five and discuss the question, "What are some ways someone has served you or you've served someone else?"
	• Invite people to form groups of three to five to discuss the question, "What barriers do you experience in developing a servant's heart and what can you do this week to overcome those barriers?"
Dress	• The pastor begins the sermon dressed in either a ceremonial robe or a costume of royal robes and crown. At a certain part in the sermon, the pastor removes the robe to reveal that underneath he/she is dressed in very simple clothing or a servant's clothes.
Environment	• Arrange your sanctuary platform to resemble a restaurant scene. As the sermon begins, a server seats a couple at a table and hands them menus. As the sermon progresses, the server fills water glasses, takes the order, brings bread, soup and salad, the main course, coffee, and dessert as the sermon closes.
Interruption	• Someone stands and tells how great he/she is. This could be done in a Mohammed Ali style.
	• Preplan an interruption from a person planted in your congregation. This person should stand up and apologize for the interruption but then say something like, "Pastor, people don't

Sermon Boosters cont.

Booster	Idea
Interruption, cont.	wash feet nowadays. Please stop talking Bible talk and give me something I can *do* this week."
Interview	• Interview a waiter or waitress. Include questions about the training they received in providing good service to customers. Ask him/her to share about a time he/she was mistreated by a customer but was able to turn the situation around by continuing to provide good service. Close by reminding the congregation of the importance of our roles as servants in the kingdom and the impact we can have on those we serve.
Object Lesson	• While holding a towel, the pastor talks about serving others and washing feet. At the same time the pastor challenges the people to think of someone that they can reach out to and serve. During this reflective time the greeters and ushers can pass a towel down each row, letting people pass the towel from one to another as they ponder who they'll serve this week.
Panel Discussion	• Gather a panel of people to discuss the events in the passage. Dress them in biblical costumes and have them speak from the disciples' point of view. Begin the discussion by asking the "Peter" character just how this whole dispute over who was the greatest started. Peter would say, "Well, James and I were discussing the whole issue of leadership and John started talking about how *he* was really the one Jesus loved the most, so *he* was the greatest." Continue the discussion by having the actors focus on Jesus' words to the disciples—that the one who rules should be like the one who serves. They should reflect on how understanding that truth changed their perspective and their lives.
	• Stage a panel discussion on "Tips on Good Serving." Include characters such as a butler, a chauffeur, Martha Stewart, the Goodwrench Service Man, and an elder from your congregation.
Reading	• Read an excerpt from Philip Yancey's book, *The Jesus I Never Knew*, published by Zondervan. On page 17, Yancey references H. G. Wells' observation that an individual's greatness is measured by what he leaves in order to grow.
WOTS	• Videotape people in your community answering the questions, "What does it mean to be a servant?" "How do you feel when you receive bad service?" "What does it take to be the greatest?"

Theme 14

Serving: Shining Jesus' Light

John 1:1–18

In the beginning was the Word, and the Word was with God, and the Word was God. He was with God in the beginning.

Through him all things were made; without him nothing was made that has been made. In him was life, and that life was the light of men. The light shines in the darkness, but the darkness has not understood it.

There came a man who was sent from God; his name was John. He came as a witness to testify concerning that light, so that through him all men might believe. He himself was not the light; he came only as a witness to the light. The true light that gives light to every man was coming into the world.

He was in the world, and though the world was made through him, the world did not recognize him. He came to that which was his own, but his own did not receive him. Yet to all who received him, to those who believed in his name, he gave the right to become children of God—children born not of natural descent, nor of human decision or a husband's will, but born of God.

The Word became flesh and made his dwelling among us. We have seen his glory, the glory of the One and Only, who came from the Father, full of grace and truth.

John testifies concerning him. He cries out, saying, "This was he of whom I said, 'He who comes after me has surpassed me because he was before me.'" From the fullness of his grace we have all received one blessing after another. For the law was given through Moses; grace and truth came through Jesus Christ. No one has ever seen God, but God the One and Only, who is at the Father's side, has made him known.

Mood  Setters

Setting	Idea
Announcements	• Someone dressed as Sherlock Holmes gives the announcements. As a detective, Sherlock Holmes was always making discoveries and uncovering truths. John the Baptist came to reveal and declare that truth that Jesus was the Messiah. • Present the announcements as an application to the message, emphasizing opportunities to be a light in the church and community. • Ask the people who are giving the announcements to sit in a variety of places in the sanctuary. Focus a light on each speaker as each one gives an announcement of an opportunity to be light.
Building and Grounds	• Construct a lighthouse out of wood or sturdy cardboard to be displayed near the entrance to the church. • Make a giant sun catcher or prism to be displayed out on the grounds.
Communion	• Set a crystal goblet that contains the communion wine or drink on a pane of glass that sits on top of a hollow rectangular box, sitting on a pedestal. In the wooden box place a strong

Mood  Setters cont.

Setting	Idea
Communion, cont.	light that will then shine up through the goblet, illuminating it. This makes for a dramatic effect that will help people to make the connection of Jesus being the Light of the World and the sacrificial Savior.
	• Shine a spotlight on the communion elements to draw the focus to Jesus, both the Light of the World and the Bread of Life.
Greeters	• The greeters wear sunglasses.
Handout	• Pass out sun catchers or prisms to each person as they leave the sanctuary. Tell the congregation that these are reminders to be lights in their world. And, just like the sun catcher, they cannot make their own light, but can only reflect the light of Christ to others.
Introduction	• The person giving the introduction enters carrying a lantern, portraying a lighthouse keeper.
Lighting/Ushers	• To emphasize the idea of light and darkness and that Jesus is the light in the darkness, hold a candlelight service. Start with a few candles in the sanctuary as people enter. During the service pass out candles and have people light them at an appropriate time in the service.
	• Dim the lights as people enter the auditorium. Give each usher a flashlight to light the way as people are seated.
Lobby	• Darken the hallways leading to the sanctuary. The greeters and ushers are holding flashlights and maybe even wearing miners' hats.
Performance Art	• An actor dresses as John the Baptist, wearing a tunic of rough, burlap fabric. He walks through the crowd of people entering the church, proclaiming, "Jesus is coming! Jesus is coming!"
Postlude	• Play the song, "This Little Light of Mine," while your greeters and ushers hand people little candles and then light them.
Prayer	• Invite people to come forward and pray at a prayer railing or at the foot of the cross or altar. If possible, light the prayer area and darken the rest of the sanctuary.

Mood 🕯 Setters cont.

Setting	Idea
Video	• Play a scene from *Star Wars* where the characters are battling with light sabers to show how light cuts through the darkness.
Visual Art	• Design a visual image of a brilliant sun on the back wall of the platform or on a bulletin board in the lobby.
Welcome	• A potter who is forming a lump of clay into a bowl or vase can give the welcome. The potter is spinning the wheel while explaining that even though Jesus is the Great Potter through whom everything is made, he lowered himself to become clay like us.

Sermon 💡 Boosters

Booster	Idea
Action Step	• During the sermon, invite someone to come forward and have his/her feet washed by the pastor. Explain that even Jesus knew his identity as the Creator of this world, he was humble enough to wash the feet of his disciples. Also explain that this calls for humility on the part of the person having his feet washed. • Produce a video of your people involved in service projects. Use this video to introduce various ways that church members can get involved in serving others. Explain that just as Jesus came to serve, he expects his followers to do the same.
Character	• Someone from your congregation dresses up as John the Baptist and reads the Scripture while walking down the aisle. • The pastor preaches from John the Baptist's point of view.
Choral Reading	• Arrange the Scripture passage so that three or more readers can present it as a choral Scripture reading. Be sure to try different techniques like having the readers repeat significant verses, overlapping one on top of another. The use of echoes, whispers, and shouts are all techniques used in choral readings.
Discussion Groups	• Break the congregation into groups of three to five to discuss the question, "What blocks the light of Jesus from reaching you?"

Sermon Boosters cont.

Booster	Idea
Environment	• Create the environment of a passport office or an airport. Both are places where having proof of identity is very important. • Use a towel and a basin to create a simple environment. • Create an environment by setting a large replica of a lighthouse surrounded by lanterns on the platform. The pastor may choose to begin the message in the darkness, with just the lighthouse lit. Then gradually turn up the lights. • Create a cityscape of a silhouette of buildings that are blocking the light. These could be in a large display across the back of the platform. You may also use dry ice or a fog machine to simulate smog. The pastor may use these as an illustration of how we all have sin in our lives that blocks out the light of the Lord.
Interruptions	• Before the service, ask several people to be ready to "pop up" during the message with a story of how Jesus has been a light in their lives.
Interview	• Interview John the Baptist to get his point of view.
Object Lesson	• Construct a cityscape out of children's building blocks. Show how the light is obstructed by the buildings in the same way that the light of Jesus can be blocked by our sin. • In the beginning of the message, the pastor holds up a sun catcher while the platform is still dark or very dimly lit. As the light comes up, he/she points out how the sun catcher reflects the light, but can't manufacture its own light. In the same way, we can only reflect the light of Christ, not create it. This truth calls us to keep our pathway open to Christ, so that his light may shine through us.
Reading	• Read an excerpt on pages 38–39 from Philip Yancey's book, *The Jesus I Never Knew*, published by Zondervan. The excerpt is an illustration in an aquarium demonstrating that, in order to communicate to the fish, you'd have to become one of them.
Video	• Take a video camera and tape a very outgoing person from your church stopping strangers on the street and asking if he/she can wash their feet. This person might have a bucket full of clean water or a spray bottle of water. It should be produced much in the same manner as some of these television commercials where the spokesperson tries to wash people's hair. The

Sermon 💡 Boosters cont.

Booster	Idea
Video, cont.	same concept could be applied, but instead of washing feet you could have someone giving foot massages. • Show a clip from the film *Pollyanna* where Pollyanna and an old neighbor string up prisms across the dining room, making beautiful rainbows as the prisms reflect the sun. • Show a clip from *Star Wars* where Darth Vader and Luke Skywalker fight, illustrating how the light wins over the darkness.
WOTS	• Go into your community and videotape people's response to the question, "What does it mean to serve?" • Stop people and ask the question, "How would you describe yourself?" • Go into the community and videotape responses to the question, "What brings light into your life?"

Theme 15

Serving with Honor

Luke 14:1–14

One Sabbath, when Jesus went to eat in the house of a prominent Pharisee, he was being carefully watched. There in front of him was a man suffering from dropsy. Jesus asked the Pharisees and experts in the law, "Is it lawful to heal on the Sabbath or not?" But they remained silent. So taking hold of the man, he healed him and sent him away.

Then he asked them, "If one of you has a son or an ox that falls into a well on the Sabbath day, will you not immediately pull him out?" And they had nothing to say.

When he noticed how the guests picked the places of honor at the table, he told them this parable: "When someone invites you to a wedding feast, do not take the place of honor, for a person more distinguished than you may have been invited. If so, the host who invited both of you will come and say to you, 'Give this man your seat.' Then, humiliated, you will have to take the least important place. But when you are invited, take the lowest place, so that when your host comes, he will say to you, 'Friend, move up to a better place.' Then you will be honored in the presence of all your fellow guests. For everyone who exalts himself will be humbled, and he who humbles himself will be exalted."

Then Jesus said to his host, "When you give a luncheon or dinner, do not invite your friends, your brothers or relatives, or your rich neighbors; if you do, they may invite you back and so you will be repaid. But when you give a banquet, invite the poor, the crippled, the lame, the blind, and you will be blessed. Although they cannot repay you, you will be repaid at the resurrection of the righteous."

Mood  Setters

Setting	Idea
Action Step	• Create an insert for your bulletin that has modern-day examples of sitting at the place of honor. Each example could have a checkbox next to it. Ask people to mark the areas that they experience throughout a normal week and challenge them to take the lowest place when they encounter these situations throughout this coming week. Include: giving up a gas station pump when you and another car pull up at the same time, letting someone with only a few items at the grocery store go in front of you, holding the door for people when entering a busy restaurant and tables are limited, allowing someone to merge into your lane during rush hour traffic, etc.
	• Challenge people to plan a luncheon at their house and invite people from the community that are struggling or are less than fortunate. This might include the single parent mom you met at the PTA meeting, or the older gas station attendant who has no family. Plan a big barbecue and have a blast. You might even suggest that a few families get together to pull this off.
	• Instead of just throwing some old clothes in a garbage bag for Good Will, take time to find a nice-looking shopping bag and tie a ribbon to the top of it. Even if the Good Will attendant

Mood  Setters cont.

Setting	Idea
Action Step, cont.	eventually takes it out of the bag, you'll have at least ministered to this person on the job.
Announcements	• Four chairs are placed in a line on the platform. Five people then come up and begin playing the game, "Musical Chairs." In this version, however, when the music stops everyone sits and then tries to give his/her seat away to the person left without a chair. The person left standing then accepts a chair. The one who offered the chair then stands, gives an announcement and then exits. One chair is removed and the game continues until all the announcements have been delivered.
Building and Grounds	• An actor portraying a person with a physical ailment sits outside of the church with a sign next to him/her that reads, "Would you heal on the Sabbath?" • Hang a banner at the entrance to the church that reads, "He Who Humbles Himself Will Be Exhalted."
Drama	• Write a drama based on this parable, but have it take place in a modern-day environment, such as a fancy dinner party.
Greeters and Ushers	• Make badges or buttons that read, "It's Good to Be Humble."

Sermon  Boosters

Booster	Idea
Character	• Preach from the point of view of a poor person who was invited to a big fancy party and what that did for his/her esteem. Describe how the host treated him/her with honor, dignity, and respect. This could be a modern-day or biblical character.
Environment	• Place an ornate chair on the platform next to the podium. Have the pastor refer to the chair as a seat of honor.
Interruption	• During the sermon, an usher walks down the aisle to a person (a plant) sitting in the front row and tells him, "Give this man your seat." Then asks him to move to the back of the sanctu-

Sermon 💡 Boosters cont.

Booster	Idea
Interruption, cont.	ary. The usher then calls to a person in the back of the sanctuary and says, "Friend, move up to a better place." This person then walks forward and takes the open seat.
	• The pastor opens the sermon by telling about an exciting banquet that the church is sponsoring in the near future. He/she begins to read off the names of people who will be attending. This list should start out impressive and get down right ridiculous. For example, the list might begin with the mayor, a congressman, and a senator. From there it could include Bill Gates, Tom Hanks, and the President of the United States. At this point an usher comes running down the aisle with an urgent phone call for the pastor. The pastor asks who it is and the usher informs him/her that God is on the phone and wants to make some suggestions for the guest list. Before the pastor picks up, he/she says something like, "I knew I should have included Billy Graham!" When the pastor picks up the phone, a person from the sanctuary loft plays God's part over the PA system. God's suggestions for the invitation list include the deaf, the crippled, the blind, the poor, etc.
Object Lesson	• The pastor starts the sermon standing on the sanctuary floor. The pulpit is still on the platform, but the pastor is not using it. After the pastor reads the Scripture text or makes a point about taking the seat of honor without being asked, an elder or deacon comes forward and says to the pastor, "Friend, move up to a better place." The pastor then moves up to the pulpit and finishes the sermon there.
Panel Discussion	• Gather a panel of people who have participated in radical acts of service—soup kitchens, Habitat for Humanity, opening their homes to the destitute, etc. Have them discuss the spiritual benefits they've acquired through these humble acts of service.
Power Point	• Use different visuals for each part of the Scripture passage. You could have pictures of a crippled person, an ox, a well, a fancy dinner party, an embarrassed person, a barbecue party, a blind person, or a homeless or poor person.

Thematic Service

Theme 16

Jesus Knew His Identity Yet Served with Humility

Luke 22:24–30

Mood ⓘ Setter

Have the leadership team assembled at the church entrance prepared to valet park for those who want to use this "one day service." Have a sign at the parking lot entrance informing people that today the leadership team is offering an optional valet parking service.

PRELUDE WITH PERFORMANCE ART

One musician begins playing the prelude on the keyboard. Another musician enters from the back of the sanctuary muttering loud enough to be heard by the congregation. He/she may say things like, "I should be playing this number; I've studied longer," or "I don't know who picked this number, and for that matter why they didn't ask me to play; everyone knows I'm the best." He/she then walks up to the keyboardist and insists on showing how it should be done. The first musician objects and the pastor walks to the platform and says, "Jesus had some words that would be appropriate right about now," and opens the service by reading the passage.

WELCOME AND ANNOUNCEMENTS 5 minutes

PRAISE AND WORSHIP 12 minutes

OFFERING 3 minutes

DRAMA 6 minutes

"The Interview" (Joel Mains, Mainstay Church Resources)*

SERMON 30 minutes

Invite people to form groups of three to five to discuss the question, "What barriers do you experience in developing a servant's heart and what can you do this week to overcome those barriers?"

ACTION STEP 2 minutes

"Donut Give-away" (on *Mood Setters & Sermon Boosters Action Steps* video by Mainstay Church Resources)

SPECIAL MUSIC 5 minutes

"Heart to God, Hand to Man" (Geoff Moore & the Distance on *Evolution*)

POSTLUDE

(Total Service Time **67 minutes**)

---

* To obtain these resources, see the resource section on page 186.

REMEMBER

- Adapt these services to fit your worship style. Choose the elements that will communicate best to your congregation.
- Don't mix metaphors when selecting service elements.
- Change the times for each element to suit your needs.
- Substitute music or dramatic elements to suit your setting.
- Think through the flow from element to element. Transitions can be as simple as a phrase or two by a worship leader or other service participant.

Additional Resources

Overall Topic: *Humility: Serving as Jesus Did*

Suggested Dramas

Drama Title	Author	Publisher
"The Interview"	Joel Mains	Mainstay Church Resources
"And the Children Shall Lead Them"	Chip Arnold	Word Publishers
"On the Street Interview: Greatness"	McCusker	Word Publishers
"Good Friday 1991 Scene I"	Pedersen & Poling	Zondervan ChurchSource
"Good Friday 1991 Scene II"	Pedersen & Poling	Zondervan ChurchSource
"Am I Missing Something?"	Donna Lagerquist	Zondervan ChurchSource
"Call of the Wild"	Sharon Sherbondy	Zondervan ChurchSource
"Somebody's Got to Do It"	Sharon Sherbondy	Zondervan ChurchSource
"Full Service Stations and Other Myths"	Donna Lagerquist	Zondervan ChurchSource
"The Legend of Givealot"	Tom Cox	Creative Resource Group

Suggested Special Music

Song	Artist	Compact Disc	Label
"Mend Me"	Big Tent Revival	*Open All Night*	Forefront
"Heart to God, Hand to Man"	Geoff Moore	*Evolution*	Forefront
"You Then Me"	Rebecca St. James	*God*	Forefront
"Didn't He"	PFR	*PRF*	Sparrow
"Message of Mercy"	Michael English	*Hope*	Warner Alliance
"Give It Away"	Michael W. Smith	*Change Your World*	Reunion

Suggested Special Music, cont.

Song	Artist	Compact Disc	Label
"He Is No Fool"	Twila Paris	*For Every Heart*	StarSong
"Boy Like Me, Man Like You"	Rich Mullins	*The World Vol. 1*	Word

Suggested Worship Songs

Song	Label
"In My Life Lord"	Bob Kilpatrick Music
"Humble Thyself"	Maranatha Music
"We Are His Hands"	Bug 'n Bear Music
"Prayer of St. Francis"	Franciscan Communications Center
"We Will Stand"	Myrrh
"They'll Know We Are Christians"	F.E.L. Pub.

CHAPTER SEVEN

Truth:
Speaking Clearly About Everyday Matters

Theme 17

The Truth About Money—*Luke 12:13–21*

Related Topics: *greed, parable, possessions, priorities, treasures*

Theme 18

The Truth About Worry—*Luke 12:22–34*

Related Topics: *God's provision, kingdom of God, possessions, trust, faith, thought life, dependency on Christ*

Theme 19

The Truth About Persistence in Prayer—*Luke 18:1–8*

Related Topics: *parable, justice, Son of Man, faith, trust, endurance, answered prayer*

Theme 20

Thematic Service

Jesus Spoke the Truth in Everyday Language—*Luke 12:13–21*

Related Topics: *greed, parable, possessions, priorities, treasures*

Theme 17

The Truth About Money

Luke 12:13–21

Someone in the crowd said to him, "Teacher, tell my brother to divide the inheritance with me." Jesus replied, "Man, who appointed me a judge or an arbiter between you?" Then he said to them, "Watch out! Be on your guard against all kinds of greed; a man's life does not consist in the abundance of his possessions."

And he told them this parable: "The ground of a certain rich man produced a good crop. He thought to himself, 'What shall I do? I have no place to store my crops.' Then he said, 'This is what I'll do. I will tear down my barns and build bigger ones, and there I will store all my grain and my goods. And I'll say to myself, "You have plenty of good things laid up for many years. Take life easy; eat, drink and be merry."'

"But God said to him, 'You fool! This very night your life will be demanded from you. Then who will get what you have prepared for yourself?' This is how it will be with anyone who stores up things for himself but is not rich toward God."

Mood Setters

Setting	Idea
Announcements	• The person giving the announcements gets continuously interrupted by a pager or cell phone. You might want to end the announcements by having an infomercial appear on the overhead video screen or a separate television. The person would then excuse himself and run out of the sanctuary saying that he's always wanted to buy one of those.
	• As someone is trying to give the announcements, he is constantly distracted by his cell phone ringing, his pager beeping, and the need to call in to work to solve a problem, etc. This will illustrate the distractions the world throws at us. End the time with a taped voice-over that says, "Watch out! Be on your guard against all kinds of greed; a man's life does not consist in the abundance of his possessions."
Building and Grounds	• Make a mock-up of a barn overflowing with bales of hay to the point that they're spilling out onto the walkway. Place it at the entrance to the church to illustrate an overabundance of stored up goods. Put a sign next to it that reads, "I will tear down my barns and build bigger ones, and there I will store all my grain and my goods."
	• Park two shiny new cars or vans at the entrance to the church. Put a sign by one that reads, "My reward for all the late hours at work." Put a sign by the other that reads, "My new tool to serve the Lord."
Communion	• Invite people to go to one of four tables that have been set around the sanctuary for communion. Station the elders at the

Mood **i** Setters cont.

Setting	Idea
Communion, cont.	tables to serve the elements. As they serve, have them say to each person, "The world tells us to eat, drink, and be merry. Jesus tells us to eat, drink and remember."
Greeters and Ushers	• Greeters and ushers dress in construction work clothes. They might even be holding blueprints and wearing hard hats. Use this visual impression to help focus people on the Scripture passage's reference to tearing down and building new barns.
Lobby	• Set up a storage locker sales booth in the lobby of the church. Have a loud, boisterous actor play the part of a salesman trying to coax people into tearing down their old storage lockers and building or renting new storage lockers for all their precious knickknacks that won't fit in their homes. • Play a WOTS tape on a continuous loop on a television in the lobby. The question posed in the WOTS is "What is of value to you?" Make a large heart to put around the TV to illustrate that the answers given on the tape are indicative of what's in the heart of the person speaking. • Place a large wardrobe or armoire in the lobby. Fill it to over-flowing with clothes and other personal possessions. Place a sign next to it that reads, "Watch out! Be on your guard against all kinds of greed; a man's life does not consist in the abundance of his possessions."
Offering	• Use grain bags to take the offering.
Performance Art	• Stage a "scene" in the parking lot of two people discussing their new cars. One is very proud and making sure everyone hears how much he paid for it and what celebrities drive the same make and model. The other is looking forward to being able to get meals to the shut-ins (on time for a change, now that he has good transportation).
Transition	• Use "Flight of the Bumblebee" as your transition music to give the feeling of a hurried and frantic pace to life.
Video	• Show the video by Steve Taylor called *The Cash Cow*. • Show the music video *Two Sets of Joneses* by Big Tent Revival.
Visual Art	• Place piggy banks all over the platform. Try and collect as many piggy banks as possible, looking for a wide variety of

Mood  Setters cont.

Setting	Idea
Visual Art, cont.	styles. These could be placed on a table or distributed across the whole platform using tables and stands of various heights.
	• Draw three large murals on three large sheets of paper to hang on the platform wall behind the pulpit. The first is a large impressive barn. At an appropriate time in the service or the sermon, the pastor pulls down the barn drawing to reveal a larger, more impressive barn. Then at the appropriate moment, pull down this sheet to reveal a grave site or tombstone.
	• Create two silos with open doors, one on each side of the platform. As you look inside, you can see that one is filled with things that represent the love of worldly material treasures and the other is filled with things that represent the true wealth of heavenly treasures (such as family relationships and knowing God).
	• Make two large hearts and display one on each side of the platform. Fill one with clippings from magazines and catalogs of various material treasures such as a new car, audio and video equipment, fashion ads, etc., to illustrate a heart that is full of the love of possessions. Fill the other with images of hands clasped in prayer, Bibles, churches, crosses, etc., to illustrate a heart focused on riches in Christ.
	• Create a large tombstone to display on the back wall of the platform or some other prominent place. Put an epitaph on the tombstone that reads, "This is how it will be with anyone who stores up things for himself but is not rich toward God."
Welcome	• Enlist two people to share the welcome time. One begins by saying, "Welcome to our beautiful building this morning; just look at the abundance of things we have to enjoy here." The other comes forward and says, "Welcome to our worship service this morning. We live in a world of plenty with a philosophy that says, 'Eat drink and be merry,' but this morning we want to focus on the inner riches of a life centered in the Lord."

Sermon  Boosters

Booster	Idea
Action Step	• Challenge people to answer the question "What do you value that's keeping you from being rich toward God?" Write the

Sermon Boosters cont.

Booster	Idea
Action Step, cont.	challenge on a card that has been placed in the bulletin. Invite them to bring their cards forward as an offering to the Lord. Close this time with prayer led by the pastor.
Cartoon	• Draw a cartoon of a businessman who is talking to his banker and wants to move his 401k into this new investment plan called a Y2K. • Show a cartoon that has been made on Power Point or an overhead of two guys polishing their new vans. One is proud of his possession and is showing it off to his neighbor saying, "This is what late hours at the office got me." The other is explaining how his van was an answer to prayer. He'd been looking for a way to help get the elderly to church and take the youth to visit shut-ins.
Discussion Groups	• Divide your congregation into groups of three or four and discuss the question, "What have you been putting off?" • Invite the congregation to break into groups of three to five and discuss the question, "What things distract you or prevent you from being rich in the Lord?"
Dress	• The pastor delivers the sermon dressed as a farmer to help illustrate the Scripture's story line.
Environment	• Decorate the platform like an expensive country club. Write a drama of two people at the country club talking about their new possessions like a new Mercedes or a new yacht. A third actor would enter and begin bragging about his grandchildren and how much he enjoys volunteering at his church. Explain that all of us can fall into the trap of thinking that possessions are worth more than family or God.
Interview	• Interview an older person who has downsized in his or her later life and describes how accumulating wealth and possessions isn't as satisfying as some might think. Have this person share some of the positive effects of downsizing one's life. • Interview someone in a high-pressure job situation about how he/she stays focused on the Lord.
Movement	• The pastor makes a point to stand on the left side of the podium each time he/she mentions those things we value that are temporal, and moves to the right side each time he/she mentions those things that make us rich in Christ. For added

Sermon 💡 Boosters cont.

Booster	Idea
Movement, cont.	emphasis, as the message is concluded, he/she lays down on the platform and says, "This is how it will be with anyone who stores up things for himself but is not rich toward God."
Panel Discussion	• Gather a panel of people of various age groups and maturity in the faith to discuss the question, "What is of value to you?" Note whether there is a deepening of those things we value as we grow in chronological age or in maturity in Christ.
Storytelling	• Relate how common it is for us to use phrases like, "This is the last computer I'll ever *need*! And I really do *need* it!"
WOTS	• Go into the community and videotape people's response to the question, "What is of value to you?" • Videotape people in your community answering the question, "What do you treasure most?"

Theme 18

The Truth About Worry

Luke 12:22–34

Then Jesus said to his disciples: "Therefore I tell you, do not worry about your life, what you will eat; or about your body, what you will wear. Life is more than food, and the body more than clothes. Consider the ravens: They do not sow or reap, they have no storeroom or barn; yet God feeds them. And how much more valuable you are than birds! Who of you by worrying can add a single hour to his life? Since you cannot do this very little thing, why do you worry about the rest?

"Consider how the lilies grow. They do not labor or spin. Yet I tell you, not even Solomon in all his splendor was dressed like one of these. If that is how God clothes the grass of the field, which is here today, and tomorrow is thrown into the fire, how much more will he clothe you, O you of little faith! And do not set your heart on what you will eat or drink; do not worry about it. For the pagan world runs after all such things, and your Father knows that you need them. But seek his kingdom, and these things will be given to you as well.

"Do not be afraid, little flock, for your Father has been pleased to give you the kingdom. Sell your possessions and give to the poor. Provide purses for yourselves that will not wear out, a treasure in heaven that will not be exhausted, where no thief comes near and no moth destroys. For where your treasure is, there your heart will be also."

Mood Setters

Setting	Idea
Announcements	• An elder, deacon, or associate pastor begins the announcements by explaining that the pastor was scheduled to give the announcements this morning, but no one seems to know where he/she is. Assure the congregation that the pastor will arrive in time for the sermon. Continue this scenario throughout the service until it's time for the sermon. At this point, announce that the pastor still hasn't shown. After a brief pause, the pastor appears and explains that this has all been planned to demonstrate that worrying doesn't change anything, and that God is always in control.
	• Someone dressed as a raven or lily gives the announcements (see under Performance Art below for a description of these costumes).
Building and Grounds	• Place yard signs with various worries written on them for people to see as they enter the church.
	• As people exit the building, release birds into the air.
Bulletin	• Take a survey of the things the congregation worries about. Write up a Top Ten List and insert it in the bulletin as a reminder of things the congregation can pray about during the week.

Mood 🕯 Setters cont.

Setting	Idea
Greeters and Ushers	• Some of your greeters and ushers are dressed in sackcloth and some of your greeters are dressed in their finest outfits. You might even consider renting tuxedos or having the women dressed in formal gowns. • Place a sign at the entrance to the sanctuary saying that all pagers and cell phones must be left at the door with the greeters or ushers. Explain that today's message is on overcoming worry. • The greeters and ushers wear two buttons. The "Don't worry" button has a sad pouty face with a line across it. The "Be happy" button has a smiley face. They wear the "Don't worry" button on their right side and the "Be happy" button on the their left side, so that it reads, "Don't worry, be happy." You may make the buttons out of construction paper, or you may order a custom button making kit from Badge-A-Minut. • The greeters may wear bright yellow clothing with the above mentioned buttons.
Introduction	• Immediately following the prelude, two people enter the platform from opposite sides. One is a worrier and the other is one who trusts God. We listen in as these two discuss what they will wear to church today and where they will have their lunch after the service. Their contrasting views will illustrate Jesus' words to the congregation.
Lighting/Sound	• As people enter the sanctuary they hear sounds of various birds. • Stage some kind of problem with the lighting situation. Have the person in charge of lighting come running down the aisle frantically explaining that he/she isn't sure what's wrong. Later in the service the sound person comes running down the aisle with arms flailing and screaming, "I don't know what's wrong!" when a microphone won't work. During the sermon, the pastor explains that these interruptions were used as negative examples of dealing with worries.
Lobby	• The lobby has its normal decorations as the congregation enters the sanctuary. When they exit the sanctuary at the end of the service, the lobby has been filled with flowers to illustrate the fact that even as Christ cares for the lilies of the field, he takes care of our needs and cares. • Stage a simple vignette or pantomime scene in the lobby depicting people who are trying to deal with stress and

Mood  Setters cont.

Setting	Idea
Lobby, cont.	worries. Depending on the experience of your actors, they could either use improvisation to dialog their situations, or they could silently act out their frustrations. • Set up an aviary in the lobby comprised of an assortment of birds in cages. These may be collected from members of your congregation. Write the passage from Luke 12:22–26 on poster board and display it with the cages for all to see as they enter.
Offering	• Use purses to take the offering. The Scripture refers to purses. • Hand out cards on which the people can write their worries. Then have them place these in the offering basket. Explain that offering your worries to God means that you're willing to let go of them and trust God to handle them.
Performance Art	• Make raven and lily costumes for two people to wear as they circulate throughout the lobby before the service or during the coffee time in between services. The raven's costume may simply be black pants and a turtleneck shirt with a hat. Using felt, decorate a dark colored baseball cap. Cut out a long black triangle for the beak and glue it onto the brim. For the lily, wear black or dark green pants and a turtleneck shirt. Make a hat out of white fabric and pipecleaners to form the petals. Tie it under the chin with ribbon. • In the lobby or on the platform, a person acts like a worried bill payer paying his or her taxes. This is especially effective around April 15!
Prelude	• As people enter the sanctuary, play the popular Jamaican song "Don't Worry, Be Happy" by Bobby McFerrin.
Visual Art	• Create a collage of words on a wall in the lobby or the sanctuary. Use different materials or colors for each word and have the words overlapping and intersecting with one another. You might want to use such words as finances, future, relationships, job security, marriage, children, college, health, etc. • Make signs with the "Don't worry," and "Be happy" symbols described above for the greeters. Place them in the lobby. Play a tape of the song "Don't Worry, Be Happy," by Bobby McFerrin as people enter the lobby. • Decorate the lobby with lilies. This would be especially appropriate around a holiday such as Easter, Mother's Day, or

Mood  Setters cont.

Setting	Idea
Visual Art, cont.	Valentine's Day. The youth of the church could offer the lilies for purchase after the services.
Welcome	• The week prior, pass out a survey that has people identify a few of their top worries. Compile the findings into a Top Ten List and have the person giving the welcome and greeting read through it using a David Letterman style approach. • Two people wear hats designed to look like lilies. As they welcome the people, they say, "Today we're talking about how to win over worry. So sit back and have a worry-free morning, just like the lilies of the field who "do not labor or spin." • Distribute worry stones as people enter the sanctuary. During the welcome, ask them to identify those things they worry about. After the sermon, give people the opportunity to bring their stones forward as a visual symbol of leaving their worries at the altar.
WOTS	• Interview people in your town or area and ask them, "What things do you worry about?"

Sermon ☀ Boosters

Booster	Idea
Action Step	• The people fill out a card provided in their bulletin that helps them to identify their top two to three worries.
Application	• Insert a card in the bulletin listing specific areas of worries. After the message, instruct the congregation to mark off those areas of concern to them today as well as any other worries they may be experiencing. They then offer these up to God as things they will no longer worry about. Have them come forward and discard them in a safe, fireproof container or insert them into a paper shredder, to emphasize that once they give these worries to God, they cannot retrieve them. • Make "Stop/Think" cards to be distributed to each person of the congregation at the close of the message. Print "STOP" in large red letters on one side of a 3 x 5 card. On the other side, print "THINK" across the top with the companion passage—Philippians 4:6–7.

Sermon 💡 Boosters cont.

Booster	Idea
Cartoon	• Use a Winnie the Pooh cartoon showing Eeyore in his usual state of worry. • Show a slide of the cartoon character Ziggy, who is always worrying about something. • Ask an artistic person in your congregation to draw a cartoon on an overhead illustrating the ravens and lilies from the passage.
Character	• Preach from the point of view of Moses—complete with robe and staff. Have Moses explain how, at first, he allowed his worries over his speech and leadership qualities to question God's choice of him as the person to free Israel. • Take on the character of Corrie TenBoom and preach from her point of view. Focus on her extraordinary circumstances and how she refused to allow worry and doubt to crush her spirit.
Discussion Groups	• Break the congregation into groups of three to five to discuss the question, "How do you handle worry?"
Environment	• Set up a corner of the platform to look like a portion of a cornfield. The pastor could preach in this environment and perhaps interact with a raven or lily.
Interruption	• Using a pretaped voice-over, interrupt the message with the "voice of God" challenging the pastor in an area of worry. The pastor could "argue with God" over some of his concerns, stating that they are legitimate. The pastor's vulnerability will help the congregation identify with his struggles.
Interview	• Interview a Christian counselor. Ask questions like "What are some practical tips you give for helping people deal with worry?" "What are some of the negative effects you see of worry?" • Interview three to five kids and ask them what things their parents worry about. Use a similar format to that of Bill Cosby's "Kids Say the Darndest Things." • Interview a doctor on the effects of worry on the human body. • Using an open microphone format, ask people to spontaneously share their worries. • Interview a person in your congregation who has had a significant victory over worry. • Interview a person in your congregation who is still in the process of dealing with worry and learning how to overcome it.

Sermon ⚙ Boosters cont.

Booster	Idea
Introduction	• A family enters the sanctuary a few minutes after the sermon has started. They argue about being late and other things they are worried about. The pastor comes down from the platform and counsels with them, encouraging them to leave their concerns with God who takes care of even the littlest things.
Movement	• Use exaggerated expressions of worry to begin the sermon. The pastor might even dramatize that he/she has lost his/her sermon notes and can't find them.
Panel Discussion	• Assemble a panel to discuss, "Where do you find yourself in the process of winning over worry?" They should represent varying life stages and points of view.
Power Point	• The week before the message, take a survey of the congregation of the top ten things they worry about. Show it on Power Point for the pastor to refer to during the message.
Sound Effects	• Play a CD or tape of loud thunderclaps at a specific point in the message. This could startle the pastor into paying attention to God's call to stop worrying and start trusting. Or it could be used in a humorous way as the pastor says, "Some people worry about everything from, 'Did I cut my toenails the right length?' to 'Am I going to get struck by lightening today?'" Then, "Kaboom!" The thunderclap surprises the congregation.
Testimony	• Ask someone in the congregation to share a difficult period in his/her life where God came through during a time of worry and doubt.
Video	• Show a clip from the movie, *The Apostle,* where Robert Duvall struggles with God over his concerns.
WOTS	• Videotape people's response to the question, "What do you worry about?"

Theme 19

The Truth About Persistence In Prayer

Luke 18:1–8

Then Jesus told his disciples a parable to show them that they should always pray and not give up. He said: "In a certain town there was a judge who neither feared God nor cared about men. And there was a widow in that town who kept coming to him with the plea, 'Grant me justice against my adversary.'

"For some time he refused. But finally he said to himself, 'Even though I don't fear God or care about men, yet because this widow keeps bothering me, I will see that she gets justice, so that she won't eventually wear me out with her coming!'"

And the Lord said, "Listen to what the unjust judge says. And will not God bring about justice for his chosen ones, who cry out to him day and night? Will he keep putting them off? I tell you, he will see that they get justice, and quickly. However, when the Son of Man comes, will he find faith on the earth?"

Mood  Setters

Setting	Idea
Announcements	• Use the Muppets' judge character to give the morning announcements. This puppet could give the announcement alone using a puppet stage, or the puppet could give the announcements together with the person acting as the puppeteer.
Bulletin	• The bulletin is designed as though it was a legal document called a writ. There would also be a separate page to the bulletin that would be designed as a prayer writ. This section would be filled out by the congregation members and then placed on the altar at the end of the service.
Communion	• Explain to the congregation that in most traditions we simply *receive* the communion elements. But this morning, we would like to have each person come forward and *ask* for communion, to illustrate that in asking, we receive.
Drama	• An idea for a drama would be to write a skit about a judges' support group. These judges would talk about all of the problems they face. One judge in particular would relay the story of this old widow woman who won't leave him alone. He confides in his fellow judges that because she was so persistent he finally gave in and granted her justice. The other members of the judge support group could be parodies of famous TV judges like Judge Wopner, Judge Judy, or Judge Brown.
Greeters and Ushers	• Make buttons for the greeters to wear that say "Never give up."

Mood  Setters cont.

Setting	Idea
Interruption	• Throughout the service a young child (5–9 years of age) keeps interrupting by coming to the front of the sanctuary and trying to get the attention of the person leading the service. Each time the youngster is told to take a seat and there will be time later to hear the problem. When the sermon is finished, the child interrupts one more time and this time the pastor listens to what the child has to say. The child's request is simple and relates to the message of the day dealing with being persistent.
Introduction	• Set up the introduction to the service by having someone in a side room knocking on the door. (He should knock long enough that it appears no one will answer.) Finally, an usher goes to the door and lets him in. A conversation ensues wherein the usher says, "You sure weren't going to give up on that knocking were you?" The person doing the introduction says, "Well, I didn't want you to miss the point. This morning we're talking about the persistent widow. This was a woman who truly did not know the meaning of the phrase, 'Give up.'"
Lighting	• Begin the service with the lights dimmed and an audio tape playing of people sharing answers to prayer. Close this time with a simple bell ringing as a call to worship.
Prayer	• Invite the congregation to bow their heads for prayer. As the pastor closes the time of prayer, he/she begins knocking on the podium. Plant a few people in the congregation who know ahead of time that this is a signal for them to join in with the knocking. Continue the knocking until the whole congregation is knocking on the pews or chairs in one loud chorus as a cry to the Lord. End this time with the pastor giving a charge to the congregation saying, "Never, never, never give up."
Prelude	• As people enter the sanctuary, they hear a collage of voices crying out for justice. These voices should range in age and gender, as well as in the types of pleas.
Sound Effects	• Set a motion detector at the entrance to the sanctuary that triggers the sound of a doorbell each time someone walks by. These can be purchased at Home Depot or Target. • Open and/or close the service with a taped voice-over of someone imitating Winston Churchill saying, "Never, never, never give up."

Mood (i) Setters cont.

Setting	Idea
Transition	• Use a sound effects tape or CD of knocking as a transition between each element of the service. This could get quite annoying, but it makes the point of persistence, just as the widow in the passage was persistent. At the end of the service, the knocking is heard again and the pastor goes to the door of the sanctuary, opens it, and a woman dressed in humble clothing as a widow enters and simply says, "Thank you for answering my plea."
Video	• Show a video clip from a biography of Winston Churchill where he says, "Never, never, never give up." • Make a video montage of answers to prayer from your congregation. Specifically seek out those instances where people had prayed over a long period of time and were able to see God's answers in his timing.
Visual Art	• Construct a large judge's gavel to be displayed in the lobby or sanctuary. This could be made out of cardboard, construction paper, or felt. • Using a graphics program like Photoshop to create a picture with the point of view of someone looking up at a judge's desk. • Reproduce the classic painting "Praying Hands" and hang it on the back wall of the platform as a visual reminder of the value of a life dedicated to prayer. • You may choose to display this painting in the lobby to get people thinking about prayer as they enter the builiding.
Welcome	• Someone dressed like a court bailiff gives the welcome and greeting. This person could begin by saying something like, "All rise, the honorable Pastor _____ is now presiding." • The person giving the welcome is dressed in a black robe and wearing an English judge's type white wig. While giving the welcome, the judge is interrupted by a person acting the part of the old widow in the passage. You may even have the widow interrupt the judge a number of times.

Sermon  Boosters

Booster	Idea
Discussion Group	• Ask your people to break into groups of three to four and take a few minutes to discuss the request to "Describe something you keep asking for." • Break into groups of three to four to discuss the question, "What causes you to give up and quit praying?"
Dress	• The pastor could dress up like a judge with a black robe and possibly even a white Victorian wig. A wooden gavel would be a nice touch too.
Environment	• Set the platform to look like a courtroom, complete with judge's desk, witness stand, American flag, the jury box, and a stenographer's desk. The pastor could then preach from any one or all of these locations during the sermon. Using each station to make a point related to that station. • A simpler version of the above example would be to just have a courtroom stenographer throughout the service or sermon.
Interruption	• An actor representing the widow in the Scripture passage would continually interrupt the pastor during the sermon. Rushing up the aisle, she would beg the pastor to just take a moment to hear her plea. Time and again the pastor would put her off asking her to come back at another time. When the pastor finally decides to give in and listen to her toward the end of the sermon, the widow could say any number of things that would relate to the passage, or she could say, "I thought you might want to know you left your car lights on."
Interview	• Interview someone from the congregation who has struggled with a problem that he/she just couldn't get an answer to and how it felt when an answer finally came. • Interview someone in the congregation who is a prayer warrior. Ask him/her to share about a time he/she really had to persist in prayer, and specifically how the Lord answered. • Explain that the widow in this passage came to the judge with her plea for justice. In our system of law, the widow would go before the judge with a petition. Interview an attorney about the portion of a petition known as the Prayer for Relief. The Prayer for Relief is the portion where she would actually *ask* the judge for what she's been seeking, and for any additional relief the judge may choose to grant. This is the time when the judge can be gracious and grant more than what was asked for.

Sermon 💡 Boosters cont.

Booster	Idea
Interview, cont.	This is the type of God we have; he does not give us what we deserve, but rather what he so graciously chooses to grant us.
Movement	• As the pastor talks about praying, he/she assumes various postures of prayer that are appropriate to the type of prayer being taught.
Object Lesson	• As people enter the sanctuary, give each person a small stone. During the sermon, the pastor invites the people to bring their stones forward to make a pile of stones on the platform, each representing a person whose prayer has been answered. Leave this monument up for the rest of the series as a reminder of a loving God who answers prayer.
Panel Discussion	• Construct a panel that consists of a judge, a juror, a lawyer, and someone who has been a victim and discuss the question, "What causes you to feel empathy after someone continually pleads his or her case?"
Power Point	• During the preceding weeks, take a survey of the most prayed about subjects in the congregation. Make it into a Top Ten List and use it in the sermon to encourage people to be persistent in praying about these congregational concerns.
Prayer	• Insert a card in the bulletin for people to sign up to join a prayer group or to begin meeting with a prayer partner. • Invite the congregation to sign up for a 24-hour prayer vigil. Make a list of concerns in the congregation to give to each participant. In this way all may be praying with one mind and continually bringing the same requests before the Lord. • Divide the congregation into groups of three to five and focus on offering prayers of petition or intercession for those in need of justice and mercy. You might even want to have some names and situations listed in the bulletin.
Sound Effects	• Open the sermon with the sound effect of knocking. Have the pastor enter from the back and begin the sermon telling the story of the persistent widow from the point of view of the judge. He would tell how the lady nearly drove him crazy coming back time after time, and that eventually, he granted her what she asked for. Then as the pastor reaches the podium, he transitions into talking about how our God is not like this

Sermon 💡 Boosters cont.

Booster	Idea
Sound Effects, cont.	uncaring judge, but is quick to grant justice on behalf of his own.
Storytelling	• Share a biography of a prayer warrior, such as George Mueller who persistently prayed for God to provide for orphans. • Tell the story of the angel who appeared to Daniel and said he was there to answer his prayer. Daniel wondered what had taken so long. The angel explained that God does not exist in our limited sense of time and that there is a spiritual battle going on that requires diligence and persistence to win (Daniel 10:12–14). • Seat someone on a stool next to the podium. As each point of the sermon is introduced, this person reads a verse from the song "Unanswered Prayer" by Garth Brooks. The pastor then expands on the point which has been introduced by the song lyric.
Video	• Create a video insert with a movie trailer or preview style. Videotape the different elements of the service that relate to the courtroom drama your service will be representing.
Visual Art	• Create courtroom artist sketches to display in the lobby or the entrance to the sanctuary. These are used to help grab the attention of the congregation and direct their focus to a courtroom motif.
WOTS	• Go into your community and videotape people answering the question, "How do you get someone's attention?" or "What do you do when you are ignored?"

Thematic Service

Theme 20

Jesus Spoke God's Truth In Everyday Language

Luke 12:13–21

Mood **i** Setter

• **Lobby**—Place a large wardrobe or armoire in the lobby. Fill it to overflowing with clothes and other personal possessions. Place a sign next to it that reads, "Watch out! Be on your guard against all kinds of greed; a man's life does not consist in the abundance of his possessions."

• **Visual Arts**—Create two silos with open doors, one on each side of the platform. As you look inside, you can see that one is filled with things that represent the love of worldly material treasures and the other filled with things that represent the true wealth of heavenly treasures such as family relationships and knowing God.

PRELUDE

"Seek First the Kingdom of Heaven" (on *Songs from the Loft*)

WELCOME, PRAISE, AND WORSHIP 12 minutes

ANNOUNCEMENTS 4 minutes

SPECIAL MUSIC 5 minutes

"Busy Man" (Stephen Curtis Chapman)

OFFERING 3 minutes

DRAMA 6 minutes

"Speak My Language, Please" (Joel Mains, Mainstay Church Resources)*

TRANSITION 2 minutes

Someone comes to the platform and says, "I'm sure you noticed that our two friends in the drama this morning had a difficult time communicating. Today we're talking about Jesus speaking the truth in everyday language. We want to follow Jesus' example by speaking clearly in the language of our sight and sound culture. Our video this morning is *The Cash Cow*, by Steve Taylor."

MUSIC VIDEO 5 minutes

The Cash Cow by Steve Taylor

SERMON WITH PANEL DISCUSSION 30 minutes

Gather a panel of people of various age groups and maturity in the faith to discuss the question: "What is of value to you?" Note whether there is a deepening of those things we value as we grow in chronological age or in maturity in Christ.

POSTLUDE

(Total Service Time **69 minutes**)

---

* *To obtain these resources, see the resource section on page 186.*

REMEMBER

• Adapt these services to fit your worship style. Choose the elements that will communicate best to your congregation.
• Don't mix metaphors when selecting service elements.
• Change the times for each element to suit your needs.
• Substitute music or dramatic elements to suit your setting.
• Think through the flow from element to element. Transitions can be as simple as a phrase or two by a worship leader or other service participant.

Additional Resources

Overall Topic: Truth: Speaking Clearly About Everyday Matters

Suggested Dramas

Drama Title	Author	Publisher
"Speak My Language"	Joel Mains	Mainstay Church Resources
"Flood Relief"	Rick Drumm	Mainstay Church Resources
"Heroes of Faith"	Robert Lackie	Mainstay Church Resources
"Never Enough"	Tom Cox	Creative Resource Group
"Keeping in Step"	Tom Cox	Creative Resource Group
"Conversations in a Field"	Judson Pohling	Zondervan ChurchSource
"Catalog-It Is"	Judson Pohling	Zondervan ChurchSource
"Early One Morning Just After"	Judson Pohling	Zondervan ChurchSource
"One Step Up, One Step Down"	Judson Pohling	Zondervan ChurchSource

Suggested Special Music

Song	Artist	Compact Disc	Label
"Even the Hardest Heart"	Whiteheart	*Inside*	Curb Records
"One Prayer Away"	Brian Barrett	*Nailed in Stone*	StarSong
"Busy Man"	Stephen Curtis Chapman	*For the Sake of the Call*	Sparrow
"Build My World Around You"	Sandi Patti	*Find It on the Wings*	Word
"Treasure"	Gary Chapman	*The Light Inside*	Reunion
"Who Makes the Rules?"	Stephen Curtis Chapman	*More to This Life*	Sparrow

Suggested Special Music, cont.

Song	Artist	Compact Disc	Label
"It Is Well with My Soul"	Bob Carlisle	*Butterfly Kisses*	Diadem
"What Are We Doing Here"	John Cox	*Sunny Day*	Questar
"Phil. 4:6"	Linnae Reeves	*Linnae Reeves*	StarSong

Suggested Worship Songs

Song	Label
"I Give You My Heart"	Hillsongs
"We Believe In God"	Songs from the Loft
"Hey Now"	Songs from the Loft
"God Will Make a Way"	Integrity Music
"Seek First the Kingdom of Heaven"	Songs from the Loft
"Seek Ye First"	Marantha
"He Is Able"	Word

CHAPTER EIGHT

Kingdom Living: Casting a Vision for the Future

Theme 21

A Better Kingdom—Matthew 5:3–12

Related Topics: *Beatitudes, kingdom of heaven, godly living, characteristics of the kingdom, righteousness, mercy, comfort*

Theme 22

A Future Kingdom—John 14:1–4

Related Topics: *trust, faith, heaven, Jesus as the Way*

Theme 23

A Fulfilling Kingdom—John 6:35–40

Related Topics: *Jesus the Bread of Life, fulfillment in Christ, eternal life, eternal security*

Theme 24

Thematic Service

Jesus Cast a Vision of a Better Kingdom, Now and Future—Matthew 5:3–12

Related Topics: *Beatitudes, kingdom of heaven, godly living, characteristics of the kingdom*

Theme 21

A Better Kingdom

Matthew 5:3–12

"Blessed are the poor in spirit, for theirs is the kingdom of heaven. Blessed are those who mourn, for they will be comforted. Blessed are the meek, for they will inherit the earth. Blessed are those who hunger and thirst for righteousness, for they will be filled. Blessed are the merciful, for they will be shown mercy. Blessed are the pure in heart, for they will see God. Blessed are the peacemakers, for they will be called sons of God. Blessed are those who are persecuted because of righteousness, for theirs is the kingdom of heaven. Blessed are you when people insult you, persecute you and falsely say all kinds of evil against you because of me. Rejoice and be glad, because great is your reward in heaven, for in the same way they persecuted the prophets who were before you."

Mood  Setters

Setting	Idea
Announcements	• Using a "kingdom" theme, have your announcements given by the king's messenger. He could come down the center aisle yelling, "Hear ye, hear ye! Thus sayeth the king and his royal magistrates. The men's group will be meeting this Saturday morning at 9 a.m. for a special prayer breakfast. Come one, come all!"
Building and Grounds	• Station several people outside the building dressed as fishermen and carrying fishing poles. Write each of the characteristics of the beatitudes on a piece of cardboard or paper and attach it to the end of the fishing line. Have them cast their lines as a way of pointing out the characteristics of Jesus' better kingdom.
Bulletin	• Create a bulletin insert that says, "This week I will focus on . . ." List the characteristics of the beatitudes. Use this insert as an action step for people to prayerfully determine where God wants to work in their lives this week.
Drama	• Ask three people to perform the Reader's Theater piece called, *In My Kingdom,* by Joel Mains (available in script and on video). The Beatitudes are wrapped around modern-day dilemmas in this powerful drama that intertwines Scripture and character monologues.
Greeters and Ushers	• The greeters and ushers dress as fishermen, complete with hats with lures. They also wear buttons that say, "Cast a Vision."

Mood 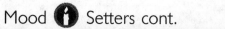 Setters cont.

Setting	Idea
Greeters and Ushers cont.	• The beatitudes are used by Jesus to describe what his kingdom will be like. Play off of this idea of "kingdom" by having your greeters and ushers dressed in king's court costumes. • Greeters and ushers could wear buttons or stickers that read, "Attitude Check."
Lighting	• Start the service with bright lighting. Gradually lower the lights as the service progresses. At the end of the service, show a slide of a breathtaking sunrise. Blow in fog across the platform, creating a picture of our future in heaven.
Performance Art	• The actors in your church create stations in the lobby where each team portrays a different beatitude.
Prelude	• A fanfare of trumpets could be used for the prelude to play off of the kingdom theme. • Start the service with a procession consisting of the pastors, elders, ushers and greeters, etc. At the front of the procession should be the cross, leading the way. • Record a voice-over of someone reading the passage. Add musical accompaniment. Play the tape as people enter the sanctuary. This is particularly effective if children's voices are used, showing our need to become like little children to enter into God's kingdom.
Reading	• Divide the congregation into two parts. Read the passage as an antiphonal reading. For example, side one says, "Blessed are the poor in spirit." Side two responds, "For theirs is the kingdom of heaven." Print the antiphonal reading in the bulletin. • Instead of having the congregation do the antiphonal reading, ask three men and three women to read it on the platform in a reader's theater style. Put the script in matching notebooks for the readers.
Tableau	• Demonstrate the passage by setting a tableau of scenes on the platform illustrating each of the beatitudes. For example, for verse 4, "Blessed are those who mourn, for they will be comforted," have someone in a pose, hunched over and crying while another person comforts him. The actors should be in a frozen pose and not speak. The lighting should be dim, with the actors almost in silhouette. At the foot of each scene, display a sign briefly indicating the beatitude being illustrated in that scene.

Mood 🕯️ Setters cont.

Setting	Idea
Video	• Create a video montage of people who are suffering, representing the different beatitudes. Add moving music such as a Mendelssohn or Shastakovitch piece or a song by John Michael Talbot.
	• Create a video montage of the same people in the above video, only this time they are receiving and giving the characteristics of the kingdom found in the Beatitudes.
Visual Art	• The artists in your church draw artistic representations for each of the Beatitudes. Hang these on the platform back wall or in the lobby.
	• Create a montage of black and white photos that illustrates the Beatitudes. For example, a poor widow dressed in black, a man reaching out in mercy to another, a child praying. Weave in phrases from the passage. Write the phrases in calligraphy on scrolled paper. Display it on the back of the platform or in the lobby.

Sermon 💡 Boosters

Booster	Idea
Action Step	• After the message, invite people to prayerfully refer to the bulletin insert that says, "This week I will focus on . . ." Ask them to spend five minutes each day this next week determining where God is at work developing the Beatitudes in their lives.
Bulletin	• Print the Beatitudes in the bulletin with a check box next to each one. Ask the people to put a check in the box with which they best relate. Ask them to focus on how Jesus wants to use this area in their lives to help encourage them or teach them to reach out to others who also feel this way.
Character	• The pastor preaches from the point of view of an older disciple, remembering back to when he first heard Jesus preach to the crowds on the mountainside. He relates that, at first, he didn't understand some of the things Jesus said. Now as an older man, he has seen that every word is true.

Sermon Boosters cont.

Booster	Idea
Environment	• Set up an environment on the platform of a peaceful nature scene (for example, a paper maché rock next to a brook made of blue gel plastic; sound effects of a babbling brook). Pastor preaches in this environment, moving to a different section for each beatitude.
Interruption	• An argument between two people interrupts the service. A third person interjects and plays the part of the peacemaker. The pastor then reads verse 9 and explains that this has been a live object lesson. • As the pastor reads the passage, someone stands up and skeptically says, "Yeah, right. That's easy for you to say. How can someone who's poor be blessed?"
Power Point	• Create a list of the top ten advantages of being poor as given by Monika Hellwig in *The Jesus I Never Knew,* by Philip Yancey, Zondervan Press, page 115.
Prayer	• The pastor guides the congregation to pray according to the passage. For example, one group prays that they may become more willing to comfort those who mourn. Another group prays that they may develop a greater hunger and thirst for righteousness.
Reading	• Read an excerpt from page 111 of Philip Yancey's book, *The Jesus I Never Knew*, Zondervan Press. The second paragraph sheds lights on why Jesus honors those the world sees as underprivileged.
Video	• Show a scene from the movie, *Jesus of Nazareth,* where Jesus is preaching the Beatitudes to the crowd.
WOTS	• Videotape people's answers to the questions, "What does it mean to be blessed?" "Do you think the meek will inherit the earth?" • Go into the community and videotape responses to the question, "What brings you happiness?"

Theme 22

A Future Kingdom

John 14:1–4

"Do not let your hearts be troubled. Trust in God; trust also in me. In my Father's house are many rooms; if it were not so, I would have told you. I am going there to prepare a place for you. And if I go and prepare a place for you, I will come back and take you to be with me that you also may be where I am. You know the way to the place where I am going."

Mood  Setters

Setting	Idea
Building and Grounds	• Near the entrance, children are constructing a house using big play blocks. They might also have a set of blueprints next to them and be dressed in construction workers' clothes. • Line the walkway to the building with facades of mansions to give us a vision toward our home in heaven. • Set up a construction scene out in front of the building.
Bulletin	• Insert cutouts of paper hearts in the bulletin to be used for a special offering. After the message, ask the congregation to write down their concerns on the hearts and bring them forward as an offering to the Lord. You may use this idea in conjunction with the visual arts display of Thomas Blackshear's painting described below.
Greeters and Ushers	• Jesus says that he has gone to prepare a place for us. Using this text idea, have the greeters and ushers dress as construction workers to illustrate that heaven is "under construction" and awaiting our arrival. • The greeters and ushers wear buttons with a picture of a broken heart. Over the heart is a circle with a slash, indicating that our hearts should not be troubled. These may also be handed out to the congregation at the end of service as they leave the sanctuary.
Handout	• At the end of the service, hand each person a key as a reminder of their home awaiting them in heaven. This could be a real key or one cut out of construction paper or cardboard. Print a key verse on it, such as John 14:3, "I go and prepare a place for you."
Introduction	• Interview kids and ask them the question, "What does heaven look like?"

Mood  Setters cont.

Setting	Idea
Introduction, cont.	• Someone introduces the service using a compass as an object lesson. Just as we would use this compass to show us the way while on an earthly journey, so Jesus has shown us the way to himself in our spiritual journey.
Lobby	• Create a construction environment in the lobby using caution signs, sawhorses, pylons, tools, etc. • Set up a display of an architect's plans of a building in process. Refer to this display at some point in the service, explaining that just as this building is in the process of being built, so Christ is preparing a place for us in his Father's house. • Set up a display of pictures of an urban renewal project in your area (such as a house being built for Habitat for Humanity). This is particularly effective if your church is or has been involved in this project.
Postlude	• Create a voice-over like the Prelude idea below, but instead have people talking about why they don't worry any longer and how their lives have changed because of it.
Prelude	• Create a voice-over montage using people of various ages talking about worries that they face. Use this Mood Setter to help tap into some of the worries that the people in your congregation face and to set up the Scripture for the day which begins, "Do not let your hearts be troubled."
Video	• To help hit home the point that this was Jesus' goodbye speech, compile a bunch of famous movie good-byes. If you don't have a video projector or big enough TV for everyone to see, try using actors to re-enact the scenes. • Videotape the progress of an urban renewal project in your area. • Show the music video, *Un Lugar Celestial/A Heavenly Place,* by Jaci Valasquez, distributed by Myrrh. • Show the music video, *Another Time, Another Place,* by Sandi Patti and Wayne Watson, distributed by Word. • Show the music video, *My Heart Is Already There,* by Newsong, distributed by Benson. • Show the music video, *Heaven,* by BeBe and CeCe Winans, distributed by Sparrow.
Visual Art	• Draw or create a mansion with many rooms. This might be displayed in the lobby or the wall behind the podium.

Mood Setters cont.

Setting	Idea
Visual Art, cont.	• Create large text of different worries and place them in the lobby, sanctuary, or both. You might want to use different colored felt or construction paper for each worry.
	• Design a backdrop of two hearts filled with objects indicating different values. For example, one heart may contain pictures or objects of earthly value such as money, cars, houses, or clothing. The other heart may contain pictures or objects of heavenly value such as family, friendships, or the fruit of the Spirit.
	• Display Thomas Blackshear's painting, "The Prodigal," on a slide or on Power Point on a screen at the front of the sanctuary. Under the picture, hang a sign or banner with John 14:1 printed on it. Set an altar or table underneath the screen. At a given point in the service, members of the congregation will be asked to write down anything that is troubling them on a small paper heart that has been inserted in the bulletin. They then come forward and leave the heart at the altar, symbolizing laying their troubles at the feet of Jesus. Draw attention to the lilies in the painting that grow out of the blood flowing from Jesus' feet. In a similar way, Jesus gives us hope both now and in the future that life can come from death.

Sermon Boosters

Booster	Idea
Character	• Preach as the character of Columbus who was searching for the promised land. You might want to use a looking glass as an object lesson. Jesus is casting the vision of a better kingdom to come. Columbus had faith that a promised land lay on the other side of the ocean.
Discussion Groups	• Divide the congregation into groups of three to five and ask them to share around the topic, "What is God doing in the midst of your difficult times now and what is your hope for the future?"
	• Divide the congregation into groups of three to five and ask them to share around the topic, "What are your dreams for the future?"

Sermon 💡 Boosters cont.

Booster	Idea
Discussion Groups, cont.	• Divide the congregation into groups of three to five and ask them to share around the topic, "What barriers have kept you from seeing God's vision for the future?"
Dress	• The pastor dresses in construction workers' clothes to focus on the fact that Jesus has gone to prepare a place for us.
Environment	• The pastor preaches in a construction site, built to look like a work in progress.
Interview	• Interview one or more senior citizens from your congregation who have been through tough times. Ask them to describe how they've seen God help them through and teach them not to worry. • Interview a construction worker about the process of building construction. • Interview an architect about his or her part in the building process. • Interview an ex-prisoner who has become a Christian. Talk about how even though his home was behind bars, his heart was freer than those outside prison who didn't know Christ. He is experiencing a better kingdom now and will truly experience a better one in the future. • The pastor interviews someone who works at a homeless shelter.
Object Lesson	• This object lesson requires the assistance of the congregation. Vases of roses are set on the front of the platform and people are encouraged to come forward and give one to someone sitting in the congregation who has been an encouragement to them. • The pastor uses pro golfer Tiger Woods as an example of someone who has his eyes fixed on the future. Before each putt, the golfer cups his eyes in order to focus on his goal and keep out any distractions.
Panel Discussion	• Gather a panel of people—such as an architect, a psychologist, and a teacher. Each of them should talk about how the concept of being "in process" affects what they do and how the vision we have now effects our future.
Prayer	• Divide the congregation into groups of three to five and spend some time in prayer for troubled hearts.

Sermon 💡 Boosters cont.

Booster	Idea
Storytelling	• The pastor preaches from the apostle Peter's point of view. This passage follows the one in which Jesus predicts Peter's denial. In this context, Peter tells of the Lord comforting his disciples.
WOTS	• Go out into the community and videotape responses to the question, "When have you experienced encouragement during tough times?" • Go out into the community and videotape responses to the question, "What is heaven like?"

Theme 23

A Fulfilling Kingdom

John 6:35–40

Then Jesus declared, "I am the bread of life. He who comes to me will never go hungry, and he who believes in me will never be thirsty. But as I told you, you have seen me and still you do not believe. All that the Father gives me will come to me, and whoever comes to me I will never drive away. For I have come down from heaven not to do my will but to do the will of him who sent me. And this is the will of him who sent me, that I shall lose none of all that he has given me, but raise them up at the last day. For my Father's will is that everyone who looks to the Son and believes in him shall have eternal life, and I will raise him up at the last day."

Mood  Setters

Setting	Idea
Announcements	• Dress someone like a baker to give the announcements. He/she relates each announcement to ingredients in various types of bread. For instance, Bible Studies would fall under the category of whole grain breads, youth activities would be under banana bread, prayer meetings would be unleavened bread, small groups would be multigrain bread, and children's activities would be bread that's still rising.
Building and Grounds	• Park a large bread truck in the parking lot. Open the back door to reveal one single loaf of bread in the truck. Refer to this later in the introduction to the service.
Greeters and Ushers	• Greeters and ushers wear buttons that say, "Pass the Bread."
Handout	• Give each person a packet of yeast to remind them that Jesus rose from the dead and is the Bread of Life that completely satisfies.
Introduction	• Dress someone as the driver of a bread truck (white shirt and pants, white cap, a name on his shirt). Make a logo for the back of the shirt that says, "Bread of Life." The driver shares that he gets questions all the time about his big bread truck that only has one loaf of bread in it. He reads John 6:35 and explains that with *this* bread, the Bread of Life, you're guaranteed never to go hungry again, so who needs a truck full of bread?
Lobby	• Fill the lobby with the aroma of fresh-baked bread. Place a large sign at the door to the sanctuary that reads, "Enter here to taste the Bread of Life."

Mood 🕯 Setters cont.

Setting	Idea
Prelude/ Transition Music	• Play the song, "Bread Blessed and Broken," from the Catholic hymnal. It's a very melodic and moving piece and will set a mood of reverence. Weave portions of this song as transitions between the elements of the service.
Visual Art	• Design a restaurant storefront for the back wall of the platform. Call it "The Father's Restaurant." Place a large sign in the window that reads, "Now serving the Bread of Life." • Arrange several baskets on the platform that are filled to overflowing with various types of bread.
Welcome	• During the welcome, draw attention to a basket of bread. Explain that it smells great and it's good food, but this morning we're talking about Jesus, the Bread of Life, and that Jesus truly fills the emptiness in us.

Sermon 💡 Boosters

Booster	Idea
Application	• Announce that today your church will be providing fresh baked bread for sale after the service. Encourage people to plan to give a loaf of bread to an unchurched friend or co-worker. Challenge them to share the Bread of Life, Jesus, during that time as well.
Discussion Groups	• Break into groups of three to five to discuss the question, "Why do I try to fill up on everything else (friends, work, entertainment, etc.) when I could have the Bread of Life?" • Break into groups of three to five to discuss the question, "How can I 'pass the bread' to those I come in contact with outside of the church?"
Dress	• The pastor dresses as a baker. He/she speaks from the point of view of God the Father, offering his Son as the bread of life.
Interview	• Interview a baker about the process of making bread. Talk about the main ingredient (flour) and what effect yeast has on the bread. Liken the flour to Jesus and the yeast to the resurrection. Explain that the resurrection is what makes Jesus the bread of life.

Sermon 💡 Boosters cont.

Booster	Idea
Interview, cont.	• Interview a "Martha Stewart" character to share "Tips for serving the Bread of Life to others." Include such things as preparing ahead of time, serving fresh bread, not loading it up with artificial ingredients, etc. Liken this to sharing Jesus with others. We should be well prepared, share our faith in fresh ways, and not dress the gospel up with artificial extras.
Object Lesson	• Place two loaves of bread on a table next to the podium. On first inspection, they seem to be the same. On closer inspection, one loaf is good, fresh bread. The other is made out of sawdust. It looks, like real bread, and it may provide a full stomach, but it has no nutritional value. In our spiritual lives, we may try to fill up on cheap substitutes, but the truth is there is no substitute for the Bread of Life, Jesus, who fills and fulfills.
Panel Discussion	• Gather a panel of four to six to discuss Jesus, the Bread of Life. Discuss the emptiness each one had before they knew Jesus and how he has filled that emptiness and satisfied them.
Prayer	• Break into groups of three to five to pray for individuals the Lord may be leading you to "pass the bread" to.
WOTS	• Go into the community and videotape peoples' responses to the question, "Where do you find fulfillment?"

Thematic Service

Theme 24

Jesus Cast a Vision of a Better Kingdom, Now and Future

Matthew 5:3–12

Mood 🛈 Setters

• **Building and Grounds/Performance Art**—Station several people outside the building dressed as fishermen and carrying fishing poles. Write each of the characteristics of the Beatitudes on a piece of cardboard or paper and attach it to the end of the fishing line. Have them cast their lines as a way of pointing out the characteristics of Jesus' better kingdom.

• **Greeters and Ushers**—The greeters and ushers dress as fishermen, complete with hats with lures. They also wear buttons that say, "Cast a Vision."

PRELUDE

WELCOME AND ANNOUNCEMENTS 5 minutes

DRAMA 6 minutes

"In My Kingdom" (Joel Mains, Mainstay Church Resources)*

PRAISE AND WORSHIP 12 minutes

ANTIPHONAL READING 4 minutes

Divide the congregation into two parts. Read the passage as an antiphonal reading. For example, side one says, "Blessed are the poor in spirit." Side two responds, "For theirs is the kingdom of heaven." Print the antiphonal reading in the bulletin.

SPECIAL MUSIC 5 minutes

"Blessed Are" (Wayne Watson on *Field of Your Soul*)

SERMON WITH POWER POINT 30 minutes

Create a list of the top ten advantages of being poor as given by Monika Hellwig in *The Jesus I Never Knew* (Philip Yancey, Zondervan Press, p. 115).

ACTION STEP 5 minutes

"Alligator Dundee" (on *Mood Setters & Sermon Boosters*, Mainstay Church Resources)

POSTLUDE

(Total Service Time **67 minutes**)

---

* *To obtain these resources, see the resource section on page 186.*

REMEMBER

•Adapt these services to fit your worship style. Choose the elements that will communicate best to your congregation.

•Don't mix metaphors when selecting service elements.

•Change the times for each element to suit your needs.

•Substitute music or dramatic elements to suit your setting.

•Think through the flow from element to element. Transitions can be as simple as a phrase or two by a worship leader or other service participant.

Additional Resources

Overall Topic: Kingdom Living: Casting a Vision for the Future

Suggested Dramas

Drama Title	Author	Publisher
"In My Kingdom"	Joel Mains	Mainstay Church Resources
"At Heaven's Door"	Drumm & Yarbrough	Mainstay Church Resources
"The Big Game"	Stephen Seiple	Mainstay Church Resources
"So, This Is Heaven"	Judson Poling	Zondervan ChurchSource
"The Right Thing"	Various	Zondervan ChurchSource
"Manna—Plain or Peanut?"	David Harrell	Creative Resource Group

Suggested Special Music

Song Title	Artist	Compact Disc	Label
"Blessed Are"	Wayne Watson	*Field of Your Soul*	Warner Alliance
"Blessed Are the Broken"	Paul Q. Pek	*Paul Q. Pek*	Absolute Records
"Heaven"	BeBe and CeCe	*Greatest Hits Winans*	EMI/Sparrow
"My Heart's Already There"	Newsong	*People Get Ready*	Day Spring
"In Heaven"	Phillips, Craig & Dean	*Phillips, Craig & Dean*	Starsong
"Perfect World"	Dick and Mel Tunney	*Left to Write*	Starsong
"Home Where I Belong"	Gaither Vocal Band	*Piece of the Rock*	Starsong
"Not Half Has Been Told"	Newsong	*Light Your World*	Day Spring
"So Much More to Come"	Babbie Mason	*A World of Difference*	Word

Suggested Special Music, cont.

Song Title	Artist	Compact Disc	Label
"That's When I'll Know I'm Home"	Geoff Moore	*Evolution*	Forefront
"Where the Streets Have No Name"	U2	*The Joshua Tree*	Warner
"Another Time, Another Place"	Sandi Patti	*Another Time, Another Place*	Word
"Un Lugar Celestial/ A Heavenly Place"	Jaci Velasquez	*Heavenly Place*	Myrrh
"Big House"	Audio Adrenaline	*Don't Censor Me*	Forefront
"On My Way to Paradise"	Bob Carlisle	*Butterfly Kisses*	Diadem
"Go Against the Stream"	Israel	*Whisper It Loud*	CCG

Suggested Worship Songs

Song	Label
"Nothing Is So Wonderful"	Vineyard
"I Want to Be Where You Are"	Integrity IV
"Holy Is The Lord on High"	Vineyard
"We Will Glorify"	Integrity I
"Lord Most High"	Integrity XI
"To Him Who Sits on the Throne"	Integrity
"We Worship You Lord"	Out of the Door Music
"Lord I Lift Your Name on High"	Marantha

CHAPTER NINE

Christ's Mission for Us:
Live as He Did

Theme 25

Mission Impossible—*John 15:18–25*

Related Topics: *persecution, Christ's sufferings, boldness, rejection, acts of service, heroes, Christian character, identifying with Christ*

Theme 26

Mission Cornerstone—*Luke 20:9–19*

Related Topics: *parable of the tenants, sacrifice of Christ, cost of discipleship, love of God*

Theme 27

Mission Hosanna!—*Mark 11:1–19*

Related Topics: *Palm Sunday, triumphal entry, passion week, praise*

Theme 28

Thematic Service

Jesus Courageously Completed His Assigned Mission—*John 15:18–25*

Related Topics: *persecution, Christ's sufferings, boldness, rejection, acts of service*

Theme 25

Mission Impossible

John 15:18–25

"If the world hates you, keep in mind that it hated me first. If you belonged to the world, it would love you as its own. As it is, you do not belong to the world, but I have chosen you out of the world. That is why the world hates you. Remember the words I spoke to you: 'No servant is greater than his master.' If they persecuted me, they will persecute you also. If they obeyed my teaching, they will obey yours also. They will treat you this way because of my name, for they do not know the One who sent me. If I had not come and spoken to them, they would not be guilty of sin. Now, however, they have no excuse for their sin. He who hates me hates my Father as well. If I had not done among them what no one else did, they would not be guilty of sin. But now they have seen these miracles, and yet they have hated both me and my Father. But this is to fulfill what is written in their Law: 'They hated me without reason.'"

Mood  Setters

Setting	Idea
Announcements	• Someone dressed as the Cowardly Lion character from *The Wizard of Oz* gives the announcements. For example, "I'm not afraid to go to that Sunday school class. I'd go there on one foot. I'd go there with one paw tied behind my back."
Building and Grounds	• Set up a phone booth outside of the sanctuary or in the lobby. In a takeoff of the television show and movie, *Mission Impossible*, have a person inside the phone booth act as though they are receiving their assigned mission from headquarters.
Bulletin	• Create a bulletin insert that challenges people to answer the question, "What is your mission?" Refer to this insert during a time of reflection after the message. Allow time for prayer as people seek God's direction.
	• Design the bulletin to look like a "mission impossible" assignment. List ministry opportunities as the congregation's ministry assignments.
Communion	• Focus the meditation of this time on Jesus' suffering and our call to follow in his courageous footsteps.
Drama	• Ask two people (plus optional extras) to perform, *Impossible Mission*, by Doug and Melissa Timberlake (available in script and on video). The characters include an agent, a person for a voice-over of a superior agent, and optional extra agents. This is a parody of the *Mission Impossible* television program. A special agent is debriefed of his top-secret mission. His assignment, should he take it, is the greatest undercover role of all

Mood 🕯 Setters cont.

Setting	Idea
Drama, cont.	time—the assignment given to Jesus. A clever twist in the script leads the audience to see that Jesus courageously accepted his impossible mission of making eternity possible for all.
Greeters and Ushers	• Dress the greeters and ushers in trench coats and sunglasses to look like undercover agents. • Make buttons for your greeters and ushers that read, "Be Bold" or "Be Courageous." • Greeters and ushers are dressed like "007" agents. They might even use language like an agent when asking people where they want to sit or when greeting them. You could also use your youth or kids to play the agents.
Introduction	• A person sits on the platform with a laptop computer. In a takeoff of the television show and movie, *Mission Impossible*, the undercover agent receives his or her mission on the computer. At the same time, we see the message projected on a screen behind them. It may read, "Your mission, if you choose to accept it, is to courageously follow Christ. If you are rejected by the world, remember, it rejected him first. No servant is greater than his master." At the close of the assignment, the computer reads, "This computer will self-destruct in 30 seconds." There's a loud bang, a puff of smoke, and the lights go out. When they come up again, the person and computer have disappeared.
Lobby	• Hold a ministry fair in the lobby between services or after the last service. Set up booths or tables for each ministry. Each person who "takes on a mission" and signs up for a ministry team receives a pair of sunglasses, in keeping with the "Mission Impossible" theme.
Prelude	• Use the *Mission Impossible* theme song from the television series.
Transition	• Use the song "I Have Decided to Follow Jesus" for your transitions. You might want to find a number of versions from different CDs or recording artists, or have your pianist or band play it in different tempos. • With the same guidelines as above, consider using "Onward Christian Soldiers" as your transition music.

Mood 🛈 Setters cont.

Setting	Idea
Video	• Create a video of your missionaries, portraying them as modern-day Christian heroes. You may show the video in the lobby as people enter, or as an introduction to the service or sermon.
Visual Art	• Display a montage of pictures of people in your congregation who perform courageous acts of service behind the scenes. Include three-dimensional objects such as kitchen utensils, children's books, a dust mop, gardening gloves, etc.
Welcome	• A person dressed up as a coach gives the welcome. This person should be dressed in sweat pants, a team jacket, with a baseball cap and a whistle. The welcome is given in a coach's halftime pep talk style, encouraging the congregation to get back in the game, get tough, and get ready for the victory party.

Sermon 💡 Boosters

Booster	Idea
Action Step	• Suggest to the congregation how they can courageously carry out their faith this week, following in the footsteps of Jesus. Make these specific to your congregation, such as volunteer to help in the church food pantry, sign up for a slot on the 24-hour prayer chain, arrange to visit a local prison, etc.
Cartoon	• Show a cartoon of a superhero as an example of someone our culture honors as strong and courageous. You may use Power Point or an overhead projector.
Character	• The pastor preaches in the character of Paul describing his trials and joys. Use Paul's experiences to help people better understand what this passage means when Jesus explains that, as followers, we will be treated as poorly as he was.
Discussion Groups	• Break the congregation into groups of three to five and ask them to discuss the question, "What mission has God given you?" Allow for the possibility that some will not know and will need to search this out.

Sermon Boosters cont.

Booster	Idea
Interruption	• Someone with a low voice should interrupt the pastor at an appropriate time in the sermon with the following message. "Hello (pastor's first name). Your mission, should you choose to accept it, is to follow Jesus no matter what. It won't be easy, but you will have the assistance of other agents in your church and community. The enemy is great and will attempt to erase you and your mission." The message can continue along to hit the pastor's sermon points. • Someone rushes up to the pastor in the middle of the sermon shouting, "The city of Toledo [or your hometown] has been taken over by aliens. We need help! We need a hero: NOW!" • Arrange for a person to stand up in the middle of the message and say, "But pastor, you're paid to be courageous. I do it for nothing!" The pastor responds that we are all called to bravely follow Christ, no matter where we are called to serve.
Interview	• Interview someone who has experienced persecution because of being a Christian. This experience could have come while in the workplace, the neighborhood, the mission field, etc. • Interview a person who is or was in the military about what it takes to be committed to a mission. • Interview a missionary about what it took for him/her to make the decision to follow Christ and the "assigned mission." If appropriate, discuss times when he/she faced persecution for the sake of Christ.
Lighting	• As the pastor begins the sermon, the sanctuary is dark and the pulpit and pastor are the only things lit. As the sermon continues and the pastor explains that we all will be persecuted, the lights start to change. The lighting will go from a simple spotlight on the pastor to slowly including everyone in the congregation.
Panel Discussion	• Gather a group of four to five people who have experienced persecution in the business world because of the fact that they are Christians. • Gather a panel of people to discuss the question, "When have you needed courage?" Choose people of various backgrounds, occupations, ages and gender.
Prayer	• Lead your people through a prayer of dedication to their assigned mission as followers of Christ.

Sermon 💡 Boosters cont.

Booster	Idea
Prayer, cont.	• Everyone holds hands as the pastor leads in prayer, acknowledging that we're all together in this mission and we'll need each other to accomplish our parts of the mission.
WOTS	• Videotape people's responses to the question, "What do you see as your mission in life?" • Videotape people's responses to the question, "How do you respond when you know someone hates you?" • Go into the community and videotape responses to the question, "When have you needed courage?" • Videotape children in your church and community responding to the questions: "What is courage?" "Who are your heroes?" "What do you want to be when you grow up?"

Theme 26

Mission Cornerstone

Luke 20:9–19

He went on to tell the people this parable: "A man planted a vineyard, rented it to some farmers and went away for a long time. At harvest time he sent a servant to the tenants so they would give him some of the fruit of the vineyard. But the tenants beat him and sent him away empty-handed. He sent another servant, but that one also they beat and treated shamefully and sent away empty-handed. He sent still a third, and they wounded him and threw him out.

"Then the owner of the vineyard said, 'What shall I do? I will send my son, whom I love; perhaps they will respect him.'

"But when the tenants saw him, they talked the matter over. 'This is the heir,' they said. 'Let's kill him, and the inheritance will be ours.' So they threw him out of the vineyard and killed him.

"What then will the owner of the vineyard do to them? He will come and kill those tenants and give the vineyard to others."

When the people heard this, they said, "May this never be!"

Jesus looked directly at them and asked, "Then what is the meaning of that which is written: 'The stone the builders rejected has become the capstone'? Everyone who falls on that stone will be broken to pieces, but he on whom it falls will be crushed."

The teachers of the law and the chief priests looked for a way to arrest him immediately, because they knew he had spoken this parable against them. But they were afraid of the people.

Mood  Setters

Setting	Idea
Announcements	• A number of different people come forward to give the announcements. After each person has delivered an announcement, someone in the congregation stands and hollers at them, rejecting what they've said. This would be the same for each announcer. The greeters and ushers might even drag off the final announcer.
Building and Grounds	• Create a mock vineyard with baskets of fruit. When people exit the building, encourage them to take some fruit and be reminded of the message throughout the week. • Display a grape arbor in front of the building. • Make a huge cornerstone out of paper mâché. Set it in front of the entrance to the church building.
Bulletin	• Since the parable is about the owner sending servants to the vineyard tenants, design the bulletin to look like a mailgram or telegram.
Communion	• Three people take their places in a tableau as the communion service begins. They are disheveled looking, as if they have

Mood 🛈 Setters cont.

Setting	Idea
Communion, cont.	been beaten up. They are collapsed on the steps up to the platform. The pastor begins the communion service by talking about those in the parable who were beaten for following their master. He continues by saying that, as terrible as this was, we remember that it was Jesus who made the ultimate sacrifice for us.
Drama	• Following the story in the parable, write a drama using a 1920s or 1940s style where the big boss sends messengers and each of them is roughed up.
Greeters and Ushers	• The greeters and ushers dress as farmers, complete with overalls, bandannas, work gloves, and John Deere caps to illustrate the vineyard motif.
Lighting	• Because of the dark nature of this passage, consider how you can dim the lighting in the sanctuary. Red or blue gels can be an effective way to set the mood.
Prayer	• During a time of prayer, ask people to consider to whom God is calling them to be messengers.
Transition	• Use the song, "Because He Lives," as transition music throughout your service.
Visual Art	• Construct a huge capstone out of paper maché and have it sitting on the platform. • Drape the communion table with grapevines. Arrange an assortment of fresh produce among the vines.

Sermon 💡 Boosters

Booster	Idea
Action Step	• Hand out pieces of stone to people as they leave the sanctuary. Remind them that they will either fall on Jesus and be saved, or be crushed by the capstone that the builders rejected. • Give people the opportunity to commit or recommit to ministry. Challenge them to ACT: A = Ask God to reveal his will for ministry for them. C = Call for information about a specific ministry or ministries. T = Take the challenge and join a

Sermon ⚙ Boosters cont.

Booster	Idea
Action Step, cont.	ministry team. Print the ACT challenge on a bulletin insert for reference throughout the week.
Cartoon	• Use a cartoon of Charlie Brown being rejected by the little redheaded girl.
Character	• The pastor preaches from the point of view of one of the servants who was beaten (see also Dress below). • The pastor preaches from the point of view of the father in the passage.
Discussion Groups	• Break the congregation into groups of five to six to discuss their responses to the question, "How do you handle rejection?"
Dress	• The pastor preaches with an arm in a sling as if he was one of the servants in the passage who was beaten up.
Environment	• Set the platform with an arrangement of unfinished home projects, such as a half-painted chest of drawers or a quilt that is almost complete. The pastor preaches in the environment, referring to the objects and how we often get started on something and give up if it gets too hard or costly to complete. Jesus, however, completed his assigned mission, despite the extreme difficulty and cost.
Interruption	• The three servants from the parable interrupt the pastor at three different times during the message. Coordinate the interruptions with the appropriate points in the message.
Interview	• Interview the son in the passage. Talk about how he continued in his mission even though he knew what happened to the three previous servants.
Movement	• Divide the sermon into three or four sections. Have each section preached by a different servant. This is a tag team approach to preaching and parodies the parable.
Object Lesson	• Have a large stone delivered from a quarry company and placed at the foot of the altar or podium. Use the stone as an object lesson about the capstone that Jesus says some will fall on and others will be crushed by.

Sermon 💡 Boosters cont.

Booster	Idea
Object Lesson, cont.	• The pastor shows an incomplete project he's been putting off finishing. He/she talks about how Jesus completed *his* assigned mission.
Panel Discussion	• Create a panel discussion using the tenants and the servants. Each could discuss the parable or a point about the parable that is central to the pastor's sermon.
Prayer	• Ask the congregation to gather according to ministry teams and pray for their assigned mission.
WOTS	• Videotape people in your community answering the question, "When have you been rejected?" You could also do this live in your congregation by prepping some people beforehand and telling them to come up with short answers. • Go into the community and videotape people's responses to the question, "Tell about an unfinished project you have."

Theme 27

Mission Hosanna!

Mark 11:1–19

As they approached Jerusalem and came to Bethphage and Bethany at the Mount of Olives, Jesus sent two of his disciples, saying to them, "Go to the village ahead of you, and just as you enter it, you will find a colt tied there, which no one has ever ridden. Untie it and bring it here. If anyone asks you, 'Why are you doing this?' tell him, 'The Lord needs it and will send it back here shortly.'"

They went and found a colt outside in the street, tied at a doorway. As they untied it, some people standing there asked, "What are you doing, untying that colt?" They answered as Jesus had told them to, and the people let them go. When they brought the colt to Jesus and threw their cloaks over it, he sat on it. Many people spread their cloaks on the road, while others spread branches they had cut in the fields. Those who went ahead and those who followed shouted, "Hosanna! Blessed is he who comes in the name of the Lord! Blessed is the coming kingdom of our father David! Hosanna in the highest!"

Jesus entered Jerusalem and went to the temple. He looked around at everything, but since it was already late, he went out to Bethany with the Twelve.

The next day as they were leaving Bethany, Jesus was hungry. Seeing in the distance a fig tree in leaf, he went to find out if it had any fruit. When he reached it, he found nothing but leaves, because it was not the season for figs. Then he said to the tree, "May no one ever eat fruit from you again." And his disciples heard him say it.

On reaching Jerusalem, Jesus entered the temple area and began driving out those who were buying and selling there. He overturned the tables of the money changers and the benches of those selling doves, and would not allow anyone to carry merchandise through the temple courts. And as he taught them, he said, "Is it not written: 'My house will be called a house of prayer for all nations'? But you have made it 'a den of robbers.'"

The chief priests and the teachers of the law heard this and began looking for a way to kill him, for they feared him, because the whole crowd was amazed at his teaching.

When evening came, they went out of the city.

Mood  Setters

Setting	Idea
Announcements	• The announcements are delivered by someone playing the part of a stadium vendor. Instead of yelling, "Hot dogs! Get your hot dogs!" This person would yell something like, "Men's Saturday Morning Breakfast! Tickets on sale in the lobby! Don't miss it! That's this Saturday!" The vendor would continue in this fashion for all the announcements.
Building and Grounds	• Tie a donkey outside the building to get people thinking about Jesus' humble yet triumphant entry into Jerusalem. • Hang a banner out in front of the church that reads, "Hooray, Jesus!" Use this if incorporating the sports theme. Use the word "hooray" as a contemporary replacement for the word "Hosanna."
Greeters and Ushers	• Give each person a palm leaf as they enter. Place a curtain over the upper third of the doorway so that people will have to bow

Mood **i** Setters cont.

Setting	Idea
Greeters and Ushers cont.	to enter the sanctuary. Print the word "Hosanna" on the curtain. • Dress the greeters and ushers as referees and have them passing out the big sports fingers referred to in the handout section.
Handout	• Give each person a paper cutout of a coin and a palm leaf as they enter. Invite them to hang these items from their rearview mirror, place them on their desk at work or on the refrigerator at home to remind them to keep these two questions in mind: "What does Jesus want to overthrow in my life?" and "How can I offer Jesus praise during the next few weeks?" • To contemporize the Triumphal Entry, distribute the large foam rubber fingers that are waved at sporting events. You can either buy these in bulk or have someone from your church construct them out of poster board. Write on the huge hand the words, "Go Jesus!" Have people in the congregation wave these at appropriate times during the service, just as people would wave palm branches during this special service.
Introduction	• Dress someone in a fine robe and a crown, yet carrying a cross. This person explains that as Jesus entered Jerusalem, the people offered him praise and wanted him to be their king. Jesus accepted their praise, but knew what was ahead of him. Even then, his face was toward the cross and it weighed heavily on him.
Lobby	• Display a group of palm trees or palm branches in the lobby to enhance the mood of Palm Sunday. • Set a scene to resemble the overturned tables of the money changers. Include a chest with coins, fine linens, and other valuables strewn about. Stage a person in the scene frozen in position trying to pick up the coins. Place a sign next to it that asks the question, "What does Jesus want to overthrow in your life?" • Construct and display sports pennants throughout the lobby area. These pennants should have the words, "Go Jesus!" written on them.
Offering	• Give each person a palm branch as they enter the sanctuary. Take the offering after the sermon as an application. Invite people to come forward to give their monetary gifts and to give

Mood ⓘ Setters cont.

Setting	Idea
Offering, cont.	an offering of praise by placing the palm branch at the foot of the cross.
	• Give each person a paper coin as they enter the sanctuary. Take the offering after the sermon. As an application, invite people to consider what Jesus would want to overthrow in their lives. Ask them to write it on the coin. When ready, each person comes forward with his regular offering and the paper coin to offer at the foot of the cross.
Prelude	• As people enter the sanctuary, they hear the sounds of sporting events and large crowds gathering to witness a great spectacle.
Transition	• Between the elements of the service, invite people to stand, wave their palm branches in the air and shout, "Hosanna! Blessed is he who comes in the name of the Lord!" Use this as a transition to such elements as praise and worship, the welcome, the offering, or whenever it is appropriate in your service.
Video	• Show the music video, *Secret Ambition,* by Michael W. Smith on *2 by 4.*
Visual Art	• Display a large crown on one side of the platform and a cross on the other. Place a silhouette of Jesus looking toward the cross between them.
	• Have an artist paint a mural of a hill with three crosses.
Welcome	• Open the welcome by saying, "Blessed is he who comes in the name of the Lord!" Invite the congregation to respond by saying "Hosanna! Hosanna!" Repeat the phrases a number of times to promote an atmosphere of celebration. Close the welcome by thanking people for coming to the service and for participating in the offering of praise.
WOTS	• Videotape people's responses to the question, "What's the most exciting sports event you've ever witnessed?"

Sermon  Boosters

Booster	Idea
Action Step	• Ask people to imagine that Jesus was coming to their town. Invite them to consider what they would lay down before him as he entered. Challenge them to look beyond the obvious, such as a coat, and to offer up something that is standing in the way of their ability to praise Jesus.
Bulletin	• Each bulletin has a small envelope that is filled with confetti. At the appropriate time when Jesus' arrival is announced, have people throw their confetti in the air as an act of celebration.
Drama	• Write a drama where Jesus is going through his Daytimer and reviewing his coming week. He covers the Triumphal Entry, the Last Supper, etc. When he gets to Good Friday, he pulls out a set of nails, prays, and weeps.
Environment/Movement	• Place a large crown on one side of the platform and a cross on the other. As the pastor preaches about Jesus' triumphant entry, he/she stands near the crown. When preaching about the teachers of the law plotting to kill Jesus, he/she moves to the side with the cross.
	• Create an environment that depicts the various parts of the passage. As the pastor preaches about each point, he/she moves through the various scenes (the donkey, the trail of palm branches, the fig tree, and the temple).
Interview	• Interview a sports figure and ask him/her how it feels when the crowd is going crazy and cheering. Follow this question by asking how it feels when the crowd is booing.
	• Interview a police officer about the concerns over crowd control at a sporting event or concert. You might even combine the modern-day police officer and the biblical story by asking the officer if he/she is concerned about the large numbers of people gathering to see Jesus enter the city.
	• Interview someone playing the part of one of the disciples. Ask him about the events of that week. Draw out the fact that the people were praising Jesus and there was a spirit of celebration and triumph, yet it seemed as though something was troubling Jesus. In retrospect, the disciple could see that Jesus was under a great deal of stress because he knew what was ahead of him—the cross.

Sermon 💡 Boosters cont.

Booster	Idea
Object Lesson	• Take a palm branch and transform it into the shape of a cross to illustrate that Jesus accepted the people's praise, yet knew he was headed toward the cross.
Panel Discussion	• Gather a panel of people to play the parts of various witnesses from the events surrounding Jesus' entry to Jerusalem. You may include some disciples, the person whose donkey Jesus rode, someone who observed Jesus cursing the fig tree, people who were in the crowd praising Jesus, the money changers and other people at the temple who heard Jesus' teaching, and/or the teachers of the law. Each person speaks only from his or her point of view and of what they observed, thus drawing out the complexity of the time in Jesus' life.
Prayer	• Lead a time of guided prayer. Include a time to offer praise to Jesus, to lay down obstacles to praise, and to give the Spirit opportunity to expose areas that need to be turned over in their lives. • Popcorn Praise Prayers: Invite people to stand and offer short prayers of praise. It may be helpful to ask a few people ahead of time to be prepared to get things started.
Storytelling/Character	• Preach the sermon from the point of view and in the character of one of the disciples. Draw out the fact that the people were praising Jesus, but that it seemed that something was bothering him. Express confusion over Jesus cursing the fig tree and surprise at his reaction to the money changers in the temple. Explain that the people responded to his teaching about the temple, but that it upset the teachers of the law who then plotted to kill him. Reveal that, in retrospect, it all made sense, because Jesus knew that he was both King and Sacrifice.
WOTS	• Go into the community and videotape people's responses to the question, "What is Passion Week?"

Thematic Service

Theme 28

Jesus Courageously Completed His Assigned Mission

John 15:18–25

Mood ⬤ Setters

• **Building and Grounds**—Set up a phone booth outside of the sanctuary or in the lobby. In a takeoff of the television show and movie. *Mission Impossible*, have a person inside the phone booth act as though he is receiving his assigned mission from headquarters.

• **Lobby**—Hold a ministry fair in the lobby between services or after the last service. Set up booths or tables for each ministry. Each person who "takes on the mission" and signs up for a ministry team receives a pair of sunglasses, in keeping with the "Mission Impossible" theme.

PRELUDE

Theme from *Mission Impossible*

WELCOME AND ANNOUNCEMENTS 5 minutes

The person from the phone booth mood setter gives the announcements. He reveals that he has received his assigned mission, "My mission is to sign up for one of the following ministry opportunities."

PRAISE AND WORSHIP 12 minutes

OFFERING 3 minutes

DRAMA 5 minutes

"Impossible Mission" (Doug and Melissa Timberlake, Mainstay Church Resources)*

SERMON WITH INTERVIEW 30 minutes

Talk with a missionary about what it took for him/her to make the decision to follow Christ and the mission he gave. If appropriate, discuss times when he/she has faced persecution for the sake of Christ.

SPECIAL MUSIC 5 minutes

"Keep the Faith" (Becca Jackson on *It'll Sneak Up On You*, Word)

POSTLUDE

(Total Service Time **63 minutes**)

---

* *To obtain these resources, see the resource section on page 186.*

REMEMBER

• Adapt these services to fit your worship style. Choose the elements that will communicate best to your congregation.

• Don't mix metaphors when selecting service elements.

• Change the times for each element to suit your needs.

• Substitute music or dramatic elements to suit your setting.

• Think through the flow from element to element. Transitions can be as simple as a phrase or two by a worship leader or other service participant.

Additional Resources

Overall Topic: Christ's Mission: The Courage to Live as He Did

Suggested Dramas

Drama Title	Author	Publisher
"Impossible Mission"	The Timberlakes	Mainstay Church Resources
"Close to the Edge"	Stan Durham	Creative Resource Group
"More Than Tuna Casserole"	Tom Cox	Creative Resource Group

Suggested Special Music

Song	Artist	Compact Disc	Label
"Greater Love"	Out of Eden	*More Than You Know*	Gotee
"Who but God?"	Wes King	*A Room Full of Stories*	Sparrow
"Drive Another Nail"	Marty Rayborn	*Marty Rayborn*	
"Sometimes Love"			
"When Love Gave His Heart Away"	Becca Jackson	*It'll Sneak Up on You*	Word
"Keep the Faith"	Becca Jackson	*It'll Sneak Up On You*	Word
"Were You There"	Russ Taff	*Under Their Influence*	Myrrh
"Tell Me"	John Cox	*Sunny Day*	
"That Kind of Love"	PFR	*Goldie's Last Day*	Sparrow
"You Move Me"	Susan Ashton	*A Distant Call*	Sparrow

Suggested Worship Songs

Song	Label
"We Will Stand"	Myrrh
"I Will Never Be"	Hillsongs
"I Give You My Heart"	Hillsongs

CHAPTER TEN

Light and Darkness: Choosing to Live in the Light

Theme 29

The Light Revealing—*Acts 26:12–18*
Related Topics: *Apostle Paul, evangelism, salvation, outreach,*
boldness in witnessing, sacrifice of Christ

Theme 30

The Light Triumphant—*Mark 16:1–7*
Related Topics: *Easter, power of resurrection, power over darkness, evangelism*

Theme 31

The Light of Life—*John 8:12–18*
Related Topics: *Light of the World, following Christ, discipleship, testimony of Christ*

Theme 32

Thematic Service
Jesus Broke the Power of Darkness So All Can Live in the Light—*John 8:12–18*
Related Topics: *Light of the World, following Christ, discipleship*

Theme 29

The Light Revealing

Acts 26:12–18

[The Apostle Paul to King Agrippa] "On one of these journeys I was going to Damascus with the authority and commission of the chief priests. About noon, O king, as I was on the road, I saw a light from heaven, brighter than the sun, blazing around me and my companions. We all fell to the ground, and I heard a voice saying to me in Aramaic, 'Saul, Saul, why do you persecute me? It is hard for you to kick against the goads.'

"Then I asked, 'Who are you, Lord?'

" 'I am Jesus, whom you are persecuting,' the Lord replied. 'Now get up and stand on your feet. I have appeared to you to appoint you as a servant and as a witness of what you have seen of me and what I will show you. I will rescue you from your own people and from the Gentiles. I am sending you to them to open their eyes and turn them from darkness to light, and from the power of Satan to God, so that they may receive forgiveness of sins and a place among those who are sanctified by faith in me.' "

Mood  Setters

Setting	Idea
Announcements	• If using a barbecue theme as a suggested outreach event, have the person giving the announcements wear a barbecue apron, mitt, and hat. • Set up a section of wooden fence to the side of the platform. During the announcements, have the "Wilson" character from the TV show, *Home Improvement,* talk over the fence and invite someone to a special outreach event: a barbecue to be held at the church.
Building and Grounds	• Park an ambulance in front of the church with a sign that reads "Contagious Christian Medical Emergency Unit." Explain in the service that it is the church's desire that everyone from the church be diagnosed as a chronically contagious Christian. • Set up an isolation tent in front of the sanctuary with a person inside. At some point in the service (perhaps as an introduction or during the message), someone explains how the person in the isolation tent was *not* being a contagious Christian. He was isolating himself, whereas we want to be contagious with our faith. • Make a banner with the following saying printed on it: "If you were arrested for being a Christian, would there be enough evidence to convict you?" Hang the banner out in front of the church. Refer to it later in the service, pointing out how, in this passage, Paul is under arrest for his faith. • A person stands in front of the church, grilling on a barbecue. Refer to this later in the service during the announcements and

Mood  Setters cont.

Setting	Idea
Building and Grounds, cont.	after the message to encourage people to invite folks to a special outreach event: a barbecue at the church.
Bulletin	• Since today's Scripture is about Paul being on trial, the bulletin could be designed to look like a legal document. • Print the following saying in the bulletin: "If you were arrested for being a Christian, would there be enough evidence to convict you?" • Create a response sheet as an insert in the bulletin. After the message, ask people to write down the names of two people they will pray for and with whom they will share the gospel.
Choral Reading	• Take today's text and arrange it into a choral Scripture reading. As it is being read have the lights go from dim to bright, and have the readers even shun away from the light as Paul would have.
Drama	• Ask three people to perform *In a Box,* by Doug and Melissa Timberlake (available in script and on video). The characters include a narrator and a married couple. In this stylized drama, we meet an unsaved couple who are living their life in a box. The box couple is unaware of the beautiful world full of light, love, and laughter that Jesus has prepared for them. A glimpse inside their box reveals their petty concerns, and a moment of revelation takes place as the lid to the box is lifted. • The drama, *These Parts* (published by Zondervan) is perfect for this theme. The skit is about people who don't know they have deficiencies until a stranger comes along who is whole. It is through their interactions with this stranger that they realize that they have needs that are unmet. In the same way, Paul was showing the Jews and Gentiles that they weren't whole until they had Jesus.
Greeters	• The greeters dress as doctors and ask people as they enter, "Are you contagious?" • The greeters dress in clothes of various occupations, showing how we must all be contagious Christians where we work.
Introduction	• Someone playing the part of Paul comes out to introduce this service or series. He is wearing a pair of sunglasses. • The week before, ask people to come to this service dressed in the clothes they wear to work. Begin the introduction to the service by saying, "Last week we asked all of you to come

Mood 🕯 Setters cont.

Setting	Idea
Introduction, cont.	dressed in the clothes you wear to work. Now, you may be wondering why we asked you to do that! Well, this week we're talking about becoming contagious Christians. And for many of us, the challenge is to be contagious where we work."
Performance Art	• Dress someone in a T-shirt that says, "I have GREAT NEWS!" The person is also wearing a large piece of masking tape across his mouth so he is unable to share the good news as he walks around the lobby before the service. Obviously, he is *not* being a contagious Christian.
Video	• Show the music video, *Mission of Love,* by Kathy Troccoli, on Reunion. • Show the music video, *Shine,* by the Newsboys, distributed by Starsong. • Show the music video, *Keep the Candle Burning*, by Point of Grace, distributed by Word.
Visual Art	• Display a giant pair of sunglasses on the wall behind the podium, or in the lobby. If your visual arts team can manage it, you might want to produce many different sets of giant sunglasses to place throughout the building. • Display a pyramid of photos of people with the phrase, "I told two friends, and they told two friends, and so on and so on," to illustrate Christians passing on the gospel. • Display a pyramid of photos (as described above), but let the focus of this one be tracing how the gospel has been passed down throughout the ages. Start with a picture of Jesus, then two disciples, and on to early church fathers and other key figures in church history. Be sure the bottom row or two contains photos of contemporary people. • Design a backyard barbecue scene to be placed on the back wall of the platform. Figures and objects may be cut out of paper, felt, or other fabric. The scene suggests a way in which members of the congregation can reach out to their friends and neighbors.

Sermon  Boosters

Booster	Idea
Action Step	• Create a deputizing oath in the bulletin that the congregation reads along with the pastor. Raising their right hands as they read, they will be deputized as spreaders of the Good News. • Pass out sunglasses at the end of the sermon as a reminder for people to be transformed this week through the power of Jesus. • Create a bulletin insert with check boxes in front of various symptoms that a "contagious Christian" might have. For example, (I can easily bring up the subject of church or Jesus when listening to someone's problems.) Ask people to take a minute and check as many boxes as possible to find out how contagious they are. Encourage them to keep the list and work specifically on those symptoms they couldn't check. • Lead the congregation in a time of prayer. Using the response sheet in the bulletin, ask people to write down the names of two people with whom they will seek to share the gospel.
Cartoon	• Design a cartoon depicting a guy who will do anything to witness to his neighbor—except talk with him. He even goes to the extreme of flying a blimp over his neighbor's house and dropping gospel tracts into his yard. (This idea is based on an old movie called *The Gospel Blimp.*)
Character	• Two pastors team teach, one portraying Paul's point of view and the other King Agrippa's. • The pastor could preach dressed up as Paul. He could also bring some rags that he explains were used to cover his eyes at his conversion.
Discussion Groups	• Break the congregation into groups of five to six and ask them to discuss the question "A lot of people just don't want to go to church. What can we do to change that?"
Dress	• The pastor starts the sermon either wearing a blindfold or sunglasses to illustrate Paul's condition after his encounter with Jesus.
Environment	• Using the theme of "Becoming Contagious Christians," set the platform to look like a hospital room. • Set up a scene on the platform to look like a backyard picnic area. For example, set a picnic table with a checkered table-cloth, a picnic basket, and assorted picnic goodies. You may

Sermon 💡 Boosters cont.

Booster	Idea
Environment, cont.	even want to include a couple of people at the table enjoying their picnic lunch. At a given point in the message, the pastor interacts with the picnickers, demonstrating how to build relationships with others in a safe environment.
Interruption	• The pastor interrupts him or herself in the middle of the message to invite a passerby to bring a friend to an upcoming outreach event. For example, the passerby could be a janitor on his way to do a repair or a childcare worker who has come into the auditorium to look for a parent. • The pastor's cell phone beeps during the message. It's his neighbor asking for more information on the upcoming outreach event. The congregation could just hear the pastor's response or the neighbor's voice could be heard over the speakers. • A few minutes into the message, the lights in the sanctuary suddenly go down and a spotlight shines on the pastor. The voice of God is heard over the speakers saying, "Saul, Saul, why do you persecute me?" The lights slowly come up as the pastor tells the rest of Paul's story.
Interview	• Interview someone playing the part of Paul's servant. Ask this servant to describe what happened. The servant gives some background on Paul before he became a Christian and then how he was different after this experience. • Interview someone who has struggled with sharing his faith and is in the process of overcoming his fears. • Interview a nonbeliever and ask what it would take for him/her to listen to the message of Jesus. (This would require an established relationship with a friend or relative and a high degree of trust.)
Lighting	• Use a spotlight to help create the effect of Jesus appearing to Paul on the road to Damascus. When this moment comes in the text, black out the rest of the sanctuary as the pastor is saturated in a bright light.
Object Lesson	• Use medical instruments (such as a stethoscope or syringe) to help people remember the idea of being a contagious Christian. The stethoscope might be used to see if your heart has any kind of irregular heartbeat—a heartbeat different than the one people of the world have.

Sermon ⊛ Boosters cont.

Booster	Idea
Panel Discussion	• Gather a group of people from your church who can talk about facing down the fears of talking to nonbelievers about Jesus. Have them discuss what fears they struggled with and how they found strength through Christ to overcome their fears. • Assemble a group of people to share how someone brought them to the Lord.
Power Point	• Develop a Top Ten List of reasons why people don't share their faith. You may do a survey of people from your congregation a week or two in advance to come up with your Top Ten List. In the sermon, the pastor should address these reasons and how they can be overcome.
Prayer	• Guide the congregation in praying for someone to whom they believe God wants them to reach out. Then pray for the boldness to follow through. • Plan a time of quiet meditation after the sermon. In the background, quietly play the chorus, "Open Our Eyes." Encourage people to ask God to open their eyes just as Paul's eyes were opened.
Reading	• Read the children's story, "Little Red Hen" by M/M Floyd McCague, published by Living Stories Inc. This is a story of a mother hen who sacrifices her life for her baby chicks. After the farmer sees what the hen does, he understands the sacrificial love of Jesus. (Note: As you read, update this 1945 book to 1990's lingo.)
Video	• Show a video clip from the film, *Outbreak*. In the film, a disease spreads so quickly that at one point there is nothing that can be done to stop it. After the clip, the pastor starts the message by saying, "What if we as Christians were so contagious that nothing could stop us from spreading our faith? By this time next week the whole city would have turned to Christ!"
WOTS	• Videotape people in your church as they answer the questions, "What's your biggest fear about becoming a contagious Christian?" or "Describe a moment you felt helpless" or "Has God ever revealed himself to you?" • Show a clip from the Word on the Street video, Volume One (Mainstay Church Resources) that asks the question, "Why don't people attend church?"

Theme 30

The Light Triumphant

Mark 16:1–7

When the Sabbath was over, Mary Magdalene, Mary the mother of James, and Salome bought spices so that they might go to anoint Jesus' body. Very early on the first day of the week, just after sunrise, they were on their way to the tomb and they asked each other, "Who will roll the stone away from the entrance of the tomb?"

But when they looked up, they saw that the stone, which was very large, had been rolled away. As they entered the tomb, they saw a young man dressed in a white robe sitting on the right side, and they were alarmed.

"Don't be alarmed," he said. "You are looking for Jesus the Nazarene, who was crucified. He has risen! He is not here. See the place where they laid him. But go, tell his disciples and Peter, 'He is going ahead of you into Galilee. There you will see him, just as he told you.'"

Mood 🕯 Setters

Setting	Idea
Announcements	• Ask three women to do the announcements in a conversational style. For example, "Today after the service, we will have a reception for visitors in room 102." One of the women leans in and responds saying, "Remember, he's going ahead of you. You will see him there." This woman gives the same response to each announcement given by the other two women.
Building and Grounds	• Make a large stone and place it next to the entrance to the building. Write the phrase "He Still Moves Stones" in large letters on it. • Make a large banner for the building or grounds that reads, "He has risen. Expect the unexpected."
Bulletin	• Design a bookmark with a picture of the stone rolled away from the tomb. Write the phrase, "He Still Moves Stones." Insert it in the bulletin so everyone can have one to take home.
Greeters and Ushers	• Greet people with the phrase, "He has risen! Come inside to see and hear more."
Lighting/Welcome	• Begin the service with the room dimly lit, almost dark. Dress someone in a white robe to give the welcome. Seat him on the side of the platform with a very bright light coming from behind him. The light should be so bright that he appears in silhouette. Stand and open the welcome saying, "Don't be afraid. You came looking for Jesus. He has risen. And if you truly seek him, he will meet you here."

Mood  Setters cont.

Setting	Idea
Lobby/Tableau	• Fill the lobby with the aroma of perfume. Stage three women huddled together holding flasks of spices or perfume.
Prelude	• Make a tape recording of people repeating the phrase, "He has risen" over and over. Some people are whispering, some sound surprised, afraid, doubtful, or excited. Use men, women, children, or people with different accents or speaking in another language. A keyboardist repeats the verse section of the hymn, "He Arose" as this tape is being played, setting a mood of anticipation. When the tape ends and the service begins, other instrumentalists join in for the chorus of the song—moving to a very upbeat feel.
	• Cue up a CD to the chorus of the song, "He Still Moves Stones," by Brian Barrett on *Nailed in Stone,* StarSong Music. Play the chorus only between each element of the service.
Visual Art	• Create a facade of a tomb and a stone rolled away from the entrance. Title the piece, "He Still Moves Stones."

Sermon 💡 Boosters

Booster	Idea
Action Step	• Videotape two scenes. One is a team of men struggling to move a huge stone. The other is the same stone being moved by one person operating a front-end loader. Explain that the men were struggling to do on their own what was easily accomplished by one person using a powerful machine. Draw a parallel to the fact that in our relationship with God, it is vitally important to rely on his power, not our own.
Application	• Give everyone a small stone as they leave the service to remind them that God is still moving stones today. He is able to handle anything that stands in the way of a relationship with him.
Discussion Groups	• Break into groups of three to five to discuss the question "What 'stones' had to be moved in order for you to see the risen Lord?"

Sermon Boosters cont.

Booster	Idea
Discussion Groups, cont.	• Break into groups of three to five to discuss the questions "Who did Jesus send to tell you he had risen?" and "To whom is Jesus sending you with the message of his resurrection?"
Object Lesson	• Near the beginning of the sermon, play a sound effects tape or CD of a loud noise such as an explosion, and simulate a power outage by turning off all the lights and the pastor's microphone. As the people sit in the dark wondering what happened, the pastor reminds them, "Don't be alarmed." Allow a few moments for people to settle down, then bring the lights back up and explain that when the unexpected happens, our first reaction is usually fear. God knows this and tells us, "Don't be alarmed."
Panel Discussion	• Gather a panel of people to discuss the question, "How were you finally convinced of Jesus' resurrection?"
WOTS	• Go into the community and videotape peoples' responses to the question, "What's the most unbelievable event you've ever witnessed?" • Go into the community and videotape peoples' responses to the question, "What difference does it make if Jesus rose from the dead?"

Theme 31

The Light of Life

John 8:12–18

When Jesus spoke again to the people, he said, "I am the light of the world. Whoever follows me will never walk in darkness, but will have the light of life."

The Pharisees challenged him, "Here you are, appearing as your own witness; your testimony is not valid."

Jesus answered, "Even if I testify on my own behalf, my testimony is valid, for I know where I came from and where I am going. But you have no idea where I come from or where I am going. You judge by human standards; I pass judgment on no one. But if I do judge, my decisions are right, because I am not alone. I stand with the Father, who sent me. In your own Law it is written that the testimony of two men is valid. I am one who testifies for myself; my other witness is the Father, who sent me."

Mood Setters

Setting	Idea
Announcements	• Dim the lights and stage two people on opposite sides of the platform. Place a lamp on a stand next to each person. Each one takes a turn sharing the announcements. As each does, he/she turns on the lamp to highlight the announcement and introduce the concept of light.
Building and Grounds	• Build a replica of a lighthouse to place on the lawn outside. Write "Jesus is the light of life" on it. • Make a large banner for the grounds that reads, "Jesus is the light life."
Bulletin	• Design a bulletin insert that asks the question, "Where is God inviting me to come out of the darkness and walk in the light?" Refer to this later in the sermon.
Communion	• Distribute candles as people enter the service. After the communion elements are distributed, dim the lights and play the song, "Go Light Your World," by Kathy Troccolli. Close with a challenge by the pastor to follow Jesus and walk in the light of life.
Greeters	• Greeters wear buttons that ask, "Are you walking in the light of life?"
Handout	• Give each person a penlight on a keychain to remind them to walk in the light.
Lighting/Ushers	• Dim the lights in the sanctuary until after the prelude. Give the ushers flashlights to light the way for people to be seated.

Mood (i) Setters cont.

Setting	Idea
Video	• Play the music video, *Never Dim,* by The Waiting.
Visual Art	• Design a visual display for the back wall of the platform. Using fabric, make the left half of the background black and the right half, white. Place a figure to represent Jesus on the white side and another figure that is coming out of the darkness and into the light of Christ.

Sermon (💡) Boosters

Booster	Idea
Action Step	• As a reminder to walk in the light of life, pass out small white stickers for people to put in places where they frequently look (a watch, rearview mirror, computer screen, etc.).
Application	• Use the bulletin insert from the Mood Setters list that asks the question, "Where is God inviting me to come out of the darkness and walk in the light?" Challenge the congregation to begin each day that week by asking themselves that question, write their responses on the insert, and save it in a journal.
Discussion Groups	• Break into groups of three to five to discuss the question, "What keeps you from walking in the light?"
Environment	• Place several different types of sources of light around the podium (a lantern, lamp, flashlight, candle, spotlight, etc.). During the sermon, note that each light source provides a different quality of light, as well as a different application for the light. Ask people to consider what type of light Jesus is calling them to be in this dark world (a spotlight to expose sins, a flashlight to lead someone through the darkness, a candle to be that first introduction of light in someone's life, etc.).
Interview	• Interview a pastor in Alaska by telephone and tape record the conversation. Draw out the fact that it is dark six months out of the year. Ask what it's like to live in darkness for that amount of time. Ask how knowing Jesus, the Light of life, can impact the lives of Christians living in this type of situation.

Sermon 💡 Boosters cont.

Booster	Idea
Interview, cont.	• Interview someone who has worked in a coal mine or developed pictures in a darkroom to share what it's like to come out of the darkness and into the light.
Object Lesson	• Cover the windows with shades and turn out the lights to begin the sermon with the sanctuary as dark as possible. The pastor then enters carrying a candle and opens the sermon by reading the Scripture by candlelight and then setting the candle in a stand next to the podium. He/she then poses the question, "Have you noticed how much light just this one candle has shed in this darkness? Jesus said, 'I am the light,' and challenges us to join him in dispelling the darkness."
Panel Discussion	• Gather a panel of people to discuss the question, "What does it mean to you to walk in the light of life?"
WOTS	• Go into the community and videotape peoples' responses to the question, "How do you feel when you have to walk down a dark street at night?"

Thematic Service

Theme 32

Jesus Broke the Power of Darkness
So All Can Live in the Light

John 8:12–18

Mood 🛈 Setters

• **Lighting/Ushers**—Dim the lights in the sanctuary until after the prelude. Give the ushers flashlights to light the way for people to be seated.

• **Visual Art**—Design a visual display for the back wall of the platform. Using fabric, make the left half of the background black and the right half, white. Place a figure to represent Jesus on the white side and another figure that is coming out of the darkness and into the light of Christ.

PRELUDE

"Carry the Light"

DRAMA 5 minutes

"In a Box" (Doug and Melissa Timberlake, Mainstay Church Resources)*

WELCOME, PRAISE, AND WORSHIP 10 minutes

ANNOUNCEMENTS 5 minutes

Dim the lights and stage two people on opposite sides of the platform. Place a lamp on a stand next to each person. Each one takes a turn sharing the announcements. As each does, he/she turns on the lamp to highlight the announcement.

SPECIAL MUSIC 5 minutes

"Heavenly Light" (Bryan Duncan on *Slow Revival*, Myrrh)

OFFERING 3 minutes

MUSIC VIDEO 5 minutes

"Never Dim" (The Waiting)

SERMON WITH APPLICATION 30 minutes

Use the bulletin insert from the Mood Setters list that asks the question "Where is God inviting me to come out of the darkness and walk in the light?" Challenge the congregation to begin each day that week by asking themselves that question, write their responses on the insert, and save it in a journal.

POSTLUDE

(Total Service Time **67 minutes**)

---

* To obtain these resources, see the resource section on page 186.

REMEMBER

·Adapt these services to fit your worship style. Choose the elements that will communicate best to your congregation.

·Don't mix metaphors when selecting service elements.

·Change the times for each element to suit your needs.

·Substitute music or dramatic elements to suit your setting.

·Think through the flow from element to element. Transitions can be as simple as a phrase or two by a worship leader or other service participant.

Additional Resources

Overall Topic: Light and Darkness: Choosing to Live in the Light

Suggested Dramas

Drama Title	Author	Publisher
"In a Box"	The Timberlakes	Mainstay Church Resources
"Something to Celebrate"	Wenda Shereos	Mainstay Church Resources
"Sam Sleuth and the Torchlight Miracle"	Tom Cox	Creative Resource Group
"Testimony"	Annie Fields-Walters	Creative Resource Group
"Cold Feet"	Stan Durham	Creative Resource Group
"These Parts"	Judson Pohling	Zondervan ChurchSource

Suggested Special Music

Song	Artist	Compact Disc	Label
"Arise My Love"	Newsong	*People Get Ready*	Day Spring
"Love's Never Been Like This"	Newsong	*People Get Ready*	Day Spring
"He Still Moves Stones	Brian Barrett	*Nailed in Stone*	StarSong
"Lion & the Lamb"	Crystal Lewis	*Beauty for Ashes*	Metro One
"Basic Instructions"	Burlap to Cashmere	*Anybody Out There*	Squint
"Dying Man"	PRF	*Goldie's Last Day*	Sparrow
"Mary Why Have You Come Here"	Degarmo & Key	*Greatest Hits Vol.1*	Forefront
"Written in the Scars"	Gary Chapman	*Shelter*	Reunion
"Heavenly Light"	Bryan Duncan	*Slow Revival*	Myrrh

Suggested Worship Songs

Song	Label
"Easter Song"	Latter Rain Music
"Father of Creation"	Hillsongs
"He Is Lord"	Word
"He Is Lovely"	1986 C.A. Music
"Jesus, We Celebrate Your Victory"	Thank You Music
"You Are Mighty"	Mercy Publishing
"Carry the Light"	StarSong
"Go Light Your World"	BNG Songs
"Jesus Is the Answer"	Communique Music
"Shine"	Warner Alliance
"Shine, Jesus, Shine"	Integrity Music

Drama Script Resources

Alexandria House Drama
3310 West End Ave.
Nashville, TN 37203
(800) 546-2538

Christ Community Church
37 W. Bolcum Rd.
St. Charles, IL 60175
(630) 513-7500

Communication Resources
(800) 98-DRAMA

Contemporary Drama Service
Box 7710-S
Colorado Springs, CO 80933
(800) 937-5297

Creative Resource Group
P.O. Box 1627
Franklin, TN 37065-1627
(800) 400-7063
Fax: (615) 595-9246

Lillenas Drama
Box 419527
Kansas City, MO 64141
(800) 877-0700

Mainstay Church Resources
370 South Main Place
Carol Stream, IL 60188
(800) 224-2735

Odd Sock Drama Co.
4 Centennial Dr.
St. Catherines, ON
Canada L2N 6A4

Word Drama
3319 West End Avenue
Suite 200
Nashville, TN 37203

Zondervan ChurchSource
P.O. Box 668
Holmes, PA 19043-9631
(800) 876-7335
Fax: (610) 532-9001

Related Books

Title	Author	Publisher
Unforgettable Sundays, Vol. I	Doug and Melissa Timberlake, Wenda Shereos, Elaine Hurst	Mainstay Church Resources
Sacred Play	Wenda Shereos	Mainstay Church Resources
Learning Styles	Marlene LeFever	Cook
The Book of Virtues	William Bennett	Simon and Schuster
Chicken Soup for the Christian Soul	Canfield, Jansen, Aubery, Mitchell	Health Communications
Preaching through the Church Year	Craddock, Hayes, Holladay, Tucker	Trinity Press International
Developing a Drama Group	Lamb's Players	World Wide Publishers
Marketplace Preaching	Calvin Miller	Baker
Spirit, Word and Story	Calvin Miller	Word
The Book of Jesus: A Treasury of the Greatest Stories and Writings about Christ	Calvin Miller	Simon and Schuster
Create a Drama Ministry	Paul M. Miller	Lillenas
It's a Jungle Out There	Gary Richmond	Harvest House
Drama through the Church Year	Judy Gattis Smith	Meriwether
Improvisation for the Theater	Viola Spolin	Northwestern University
Preaching and Teaching with Imagination	Warren Wiersbe	Victor
The Power of Story	Leighton Ford	Navpress

Video Resources

Title	Contents	Publisher
2000 Adventure Dramas Video	8 Dramas for Worship Services, Small Groups, and Drama Teams	Mainstay
2000 Mood Setters and Sermon Boosters Video	WOTS, Author Interviews, Action Steps, Visual Scripture Readings	Mainstay
Worship and Sermon Boosters for Promises Worth Keeping	WOTS, Author Interviews, Action Steps, Visual Scripture Readings	Mainstay
Adventure Dramas "Untapped Miracles"	9 Dramas for Worship Services, Small Groups, and Drama Teams	Mainstay
Adventure Promotional Video for "Untapped Miracles for Tapped Out Christians"	20 Word on the Street Segments (WOTS), Adventure promo spots, half-hour interview with Sheila Walsh former cohost of The 700 Club.	Mainstay
Worship and Sermon Boosters for "Making Christmas Meaningful"	Music Videos, Video Montages, Interviews	Mainstay
"Adventure Acts"—Spiritual Adventure Dramas for "The Church You've Always Longed For"	9 Dramas for Worship Services, Small Groups, and Drama Teams	Mainstay
Advent Worship Sampler Video: "The Christmas You've Always Longed For"	Monologues, Dramatic Scripture Readings and Christmas WOTS	Mainstay
1996 Adventure Dramas: "What To Do When You Don't Know What To Do"	9 Dramas for Worship Services, Small Groups, and Drama Teams	Mainstay
Adventure Dramas "Promises Worth Keeping"	9 Dramas for Worship Services, Small Groups, and Drama Teams	Mainstay

More Resources
from Mainstay Church Resources

The Little Scripture Pack for Practicing Purity
25 Fantastic Questions That Get Beyond "How Are You"?
The Real Deal Edge TV Video

These resources can be ordered through:
Mainstay Church Resources
P. O. Box 30
Wheaton, IL 60189

Or call (800) 224-2735 (U.S.) or (800) 461-4114 (Canada).

UNFORGETTABLE
SUNDAYS
SUPER ★ SEMINARS

I t's hard to stay fresh and relevant in church 52 weeks of the year. But it doesn't have to be that way. You can be effective, creative communicators every week. Our Super Seminar will get you started. **A few short hours in an Unforgettable Sundays Super Seminar will:**

► Prime your creative pump with ideas that will stretch you to think divergently.

► Introduce you to attention-getting Sermon Boosters that will help you preach more effectively.

► Captivate you with innovative Mood Setters that will set the tone for your Sunday services.

► Equip you to use simple yet effective methods of dramatic communication, like choral readings and readers' theater.

► Teach you to plan thematic worship services that support your sermon and drive home each Sunday's message.

► Learn how to make your Sundays unforgettable!

To schedule an
Unforgettable Sundays Super Seminar,
call 1-303-791-1391.

NEXT STEP DRAMA
WORKSHOPS
WITH WENDA SHEREOS

Get DrAMA Going and Keep It Growing

A drama ministry is a great way to minister to both believers and seekers. **NEXT STEP** drama workshops can help!

A prime opportunity for lay people to receive training in acting, directing, and team building from a seasoned professional, the workshops will get drama going in your church and keep it growing.

If you don't yet have a drama ministry, the **NEXT STEP** team will plant the vision for drama as a ministry in your church whether your worship style is liturgical, traditional, contemporary, or seeker targeted.

Wenda Shereos presents church dramas with her cast at the Hope Evangelical Free Church in Springfield, Illinois. Dramas provide a place for ministry for the creative people in your church, Wenda says.

To schedule the NEXT STEP for your church,
call 1-303-791-1391

Comedy Café

A Night of Wholesome Hilarity

A Comedy Café with Doug and Melissa Timberlake is a night of wholesome hilarity that your entire church and their friends can laugh along with. Doug and Melissa skillfully lead your guests through a series of interactive improvisational games. That's right, the people who attend your Comedy Café are actually on stage with the Timberlakes performing any number of crazy, zany, and always hysterical, off-the-cuff skits.

Comedy Cafés are proven, delightful occasions to enjoy with neighbors, co-workers, and friends. Take advantage of this unique ministry opportunity to ask others to step through the doors of your church and discover that it's a great place to be!

With over 15 years of performance and television experience, the Timberlakes lead audiences with an "everybody in the water at the same time" approach. Nothing intimidating, just a good chance to roar with laughter at yourself and those around you.

Invite Doug and Melissa Timberlake to perform a Comedy Café in your church and then get ready to giggle, snort, and bellyache as your congregation gets in touch with their contagious creativity and sense of humor.

Interactive Improv Games

★ The Human Orchestra
★ Clue—A Who Done It Game
★ 1950s Traveling Soap Opera
★ Dr. Know It All
★ Unusual Uses for Usual Objects

Perfect for Your Church's . . .

★ Community Outreach Events
★ Fundraiser Kickoff Nights
★ Appreciation Night for Volunteers
★ Church Celebrations/Anniversaries
★ Seasonal Celebration Gatherings

For Booking Information Contact Tammy Burklin at 1-303-791-1391

Index

Dramas

Mood Setters

Related Topics

Scripture

Sermon Boosters

Service Elements

Special Music

Thematic Services

Themes

Doug and Melissa Timberlake met at Miami University of Ohio where they were both theater majors. Since that time, they have used their drama training and creative communication skills to serve the church. While studying at Asbury Seminary, they toured the churches in the middle south performing *Mountain Top*. Since working at The Chapel Ministries, they have been involved extensively in national daily radio and television broadcasting. Both write, direct, and produce video productions for the 50-Day Spiritual Adventures, which are used annually in some 4,000 churches and by hundreds of thousands of participants. The Timberlakes have founded several improvisational groups and now conduct *Comedy Cafés*—events of laughter designed as outreach events for seekers.

Wenda Shereos is a professional actress, singer, producer, director, and writer. The Director of the Worship Programming Team at Hope Evangelical Free Church in Springfield, Illinois, she also heads *Prologue,* Hope's drama team. Wenda is a pastor's wife and holds a master's degree in communication. She is the founder and Executive Director of Next Step Drama Ministries.

Elaine Hurst is a creative consultant on the programming team at Hope Free Church in Springfield, Illinois, where she has served in this position since 1990. That role has provided her with years of hands-on experience in thematic worship planning. As a musician, she has toured nationally as stage manager with Christian recording artists Brian Duncan, Russ Taff, and Sheila Walsh—among others. Her passion is to work with local churches to help in the discovery of innovative ways to communicate the truth of Scripture with relevance to today's culture and to create "moments" that last a lifetime.